Weber: A Short Introduction

Gianfranco Poggi

polity

First published in 2006 by Polity Press
Reprinted 2007, 2008

Polity Press
65 Bridge Street
Cambridge CB2 1UR, UK

Polity Press
350 Main Street
Malden, MA 02148, USA

ISBN: 978-0-7456-3489-0
ISBN: 978-0-7456-3490-6 (pb)

A catalogue record for this book is available from the British Library.

Typeset in 10.5 on 12 pt Sabon
by Servis Filmsetting Ltd, Manchester

The publisher has used its best endeavours to ensure that the URLs for external websites referred to in this book are correct and active at the time of going to press. However, the publisher has no responsibility for the websites and can make no guarantee that a site will remain live or that the content is or will remain appropriate.

Every effort has been made to trace all copyright holders, but if any have been inadvertently overlooked the publishers will be pleased to include any necessary credits in any subsequent reprint or edition.

For further information on Polity, visit our website: www.polity.co.uk

Contents

Preface

When I started writing this book, rather too long ago, I intended my introduction to Max Weber's sociological thought to have three characteristics. It should be comprehensive, that is, address a relatively large number of the many, many themes contributed to by Weber. It should be written as clearly as possible, dealing with the topics in my own words, rather than resorting frequently to quotations from Weber's writings, seeking instead to encourage readers to make their own contact with those. Finally, it should be a short book.

I am sure only of having attained this last aim. I hope that in doing so I have not fallen into the trap the ancients characterized as *brevis esse laboro, obscurus fio* – I work at being brief, and I become obscure. In other words, I hope I have expressed myself as directly and plainly as the matter allows. But I have definitely abandoned the first aim. The treatment of Weber's sociological thought that follows is highly selective, and leaves out several topics it should have addressed in order to be reasonably comprehensive. I do not discuss, or discuss too briefly, for instance, charisma, prophecy, the city, the market and the law. Thus, whereas at one point I conceived of this as a book that would accompany readers in an *itinerary through* the work of Weber, actually it seeks at best to lead them to an *encounter with* that work.

Seeing this acknowledgement of several, substantive thematic gaps in this book, prospective readers may ask *what* it actually deals with. I answer as follows. It opens with a look at Max Weber's 'life and works'. The second chapter deals, unavoidably, with his conception of the cultural and social sciences. I say 'unavoidably' because I would have gladly omitted this chapter, which has philosophical implications I would prefer to avoid. Furthermore, some of its themes (in particular, the problems of value judgements and of 'ideal types') have been raised and discussed to excess, not so much by Weber as by his commentators and critics, and not always with much justification or worthwhile result. Personally, in my teaching I have always found it more rewarding to deal instead with the less obvious topic of the next chapter (3), that is, with Weber's conception of the socio-historical process.

The chapters just mentioned (2 and 3), in turn, serve largely as a backdrop for two great themes, which we might call substantive, and occupy the remainder of the book. Chapters 4 and 5 approach the first of those themes, religion, though they do so by starting from Weber's own interest in economic phenomena. This perspective shapes and limits my treatment, which emphasizes not so much Weber's sociology of the religious phenomenon in general as his comparative-historical sociology of religions. Furthermore, this is again treated in a selective manner, for only Calvinism and, to a lesser extent, Confucianism are discussed.

A second great theme – politics – is the subject of the last two chapters. Chapter 6 seeks to locate the topic of legitimacy and its types within a broader discussion of political phenomena, and to that extent differs somewhat from their treatment by others. Chapter 7 approaches a topic I have dealt with in other books – the modern state – and highlights some of Weber's contributions to its treatment. It also discusses bureaucracy, which one may consider in turn as an expression (present not only in the political sphere) of a broader phenomenon, mentioned also in other chapters – the rationalization process.

As I have done in other books on 'classical' authors, again in this one I have tried to stick to a given author's own writings (as I interpret them, of course) and have made exceedingly few references to accounts and critiques of writings by other scholars. A select bibliography seeks to remedy this omission, suggesting to the reader a few titles from within the large body of literature in English that deals with Weber.

Again, this book is like others of mine in that it follows a treatment of Weber which I have offered in my classes at various academic locations – Edinburgh, Charlottesville (Virginia), Fiesole, Hobart and, lately, Trento. Perhaps the fact that my writing has developed from my teaching accounts for the highly selective nature of this book, together with rather scant attention to secondary literature. That same fact, of course, means that I am indebted to many more colleagues and students, from all those locations, than I could possibly mention.

However, I would like to acknowledge four universities in four different countries (the Universities of Glasgow, British Columbia, L'Aquila and New South Wales) where I had pleasant and productive research-and-writing stays between 2001 and 2004 – the rather too long time span over which this book came to be written. Finally, I am particularly grateful to the Faculty of Law of the University of New South Wales, Sydney, for a fellowship which has allowed me to translate into English a book originally written in Italian, in a particularly friendly and helpful environment.

Università di Trento

1
The Man and His Work

Contexts: domestic and public

Max Weber was born in Erfurt, a town in the Prussian region of Thuringia, in 1864, and was the first of eight children. The Webers were Lutherans, but his mother, Helene Fallenstein, descended from a Huguenot family, and her religiosity had a sincere and austere quality that her worldly and domineering husband (Max Weber Senior) did not share or appreciate. As a distinguished lawyer, he belonged to the professional elite of the German bourgeoisie, while his brother Carl belonged to its business component, for he owned and managed a textile firm in Bielefeld.

On his mother's side Weber was related to the Souchays, a very wealthy Huguenot commercial dynasty, active in several countries; on this account Weber's persistent intellectual interest in economic matters was rooted in his parentage. The same can be said of his identity as a scholar, for law – which Max Junior, following his father, studied at university – was a particularly demanding and prestigious academic discipline in Germany at that time. Through his father, Weber soon became acquainted with important members of the Prussian academic estate, many of whom were jurists.

The intense interest the younger Max took in political affairs also had its roots in the family connections, for the elder Max held important positions in public administration, at first in the provinces, and subsequently in the Prussian capital, Berlin. He was also active in a bourgeois political party, and associated with significant members of the Prussian political class. As for his son, perhaps one should speak not only of an intense interest in political affairs, but rather of a true passion for politics, originating in the family context but also reflecting the significance of events taking place in the public sphere.

At the age of six, Max Weber was keenly aware of those world events, when Germany, under the hegemony of Prussia, and thanks chiefly to the political genius of Otto von Bismarck, became politically unified as an empire (the Reich). In 1871 the Prussian royal dynasty of the Hohenzollern adopted the imperial title. Subsequently, it sought to extend the authoritarian understanding of its ruling prerogatives, which it had successfully practised in Prussia, to the broader and more complex context of the empire.

However, the Prussian territories on both sides of the River Elbe had a socio-economic structure and a political culture which appeared relatively backward in comparison with other parts of the Reich, such as the Rhine regions or Bavaria. Where some of those parts had long been annexed by Prussia itself, the country's leaders had recently undertaken a rapid and successful process of economic and intellectual modernization in its own core regions, beginning with Berlin. For all that, the Prussian political class was dominated by the Junkers, that is, by aristocratic landowners who were active both in the military and in public administration, thoroughly committed to the Hohenzollerns' traditionalist understanding of rulership, and to the preservation of the socio-economic status quo during the modernization process itself.

As a result, in the last decades of the nineteenth century German public life had a peculiarly authoritarian cast. It appealed chiefly to conservative values of obedience, unity and shared dedication to national interests. These, however, were not to be defined through the contention of parties, but were seen as represented by the monarch and all he stood for. Chief among those interests was the increase in the military and economic might of the German nation, which through unification had become a major European power, destined to play a key role in world politics.

Both the old and the young Max Webers were ardent German nationalists. Both their generations considered German unification a historical event of the greatest magnitude, and felt a keen admiration and gratitude for its protagonists – Prussia, its army and its administration, Bismarck, and the Hohenzollern dynasty. The latter generation, however, took greater notice of the fact that at the end of the nineteenth and the beginning of the twentieth centuries, the German political system represented something of an anomaly if compared with other dominant European powers, such as Britain and France, with which it had to contend in the international context. A recent biography of Hitler characterizes this anomaly as follows:

> The constitutional framework of the German Reich [differed] sharply in key respects from that of Britain and France, whose differently structured but relatively flexible parliamentary democracies offered better potential to cope with the social and political demands arising from rapid economic change. In Germany, the growth of party-political pluralism, which found its representation in the Reichstag, had not been translated into parliamentary democracy. Powerful vested interests – big landowners (most of them belonging to the aristocracy), the officer corps of the army, the upper echelons of the state bureaucracy, even most of the Reichstag parties – continued to block this. The Reich chancellor remained the appointee of the Kaiser, who could make or break him whatever the respective strength of Reichstag parties. The government itself stood above the Reichstag, independent (at least in theory) of party politics. Whole tracts of policy, especially on foreign and military matters, lay outside parliamentary control. Power was jealously guarded, in the face of mounting pressures for radical change, by the beleaguered forces of the old order. Some of these, increasingly fearful of revolution, were prepared even to contemplate war as a way of holding on to their power and fending off the threat of socialism. (Kershaw 1999: 74)

In those decades of the so-called Wilhelmine era (named after the last Hohenzollern dynast, Wilhelm II, who reigned both as King of Prussia and as German Emperor between 1888 and 1918), the problems – both domestic and international – which confronted the German Reich led to the question as to whether its peculiar political institutions constituted a resource or a liability for the German empire. One could say

that Max Weber Senior would have given the first answer to
that question. At first his son may have shared that view, but
as he grew up he became increasingly aware of the negative
aspects of the German situation.

Weber's studies

In 1869, shortly before unification, Max Weber Senior left
Erfurt with his family for Berlin, to take up an important post
in the administration of the capital, where he was also to hold
elective positions as a member of the national-liberal party.
Thus it was in Berlin that his son's pre-university education
was undertaken. In 1882, however, he enrolled as a student at
the University of Heidelberg, in the western part of the Reich,
and there he attended courses chiefly in the faculty of law. The
following year was spent in Strassburg, doing his military
service but also spending time with the Baumgarten, an academic family to whom he was related on his mother's side. For
the next several years he continued his military training at successive camps until he qualified as an officer in the reserve
army – a title of which he was very proud. Through his experiences both as a trainee officer, and as a member of a student
corporation (*Alemannia*), he toughened himself physically
and learned to fence.

In 1884, following the medieval tradition of the 'wandering
scholar', Weber moved to the University of Berlin and subsequently (1885–6) to that of Göttingen. Here he completed his
studies and prepared for examinations which in due course
qualified him as a Referendar – the entry-level position for
those aspiring, as he did, to a career as a lawyer. In order to
prepare for further exams, he returned to the family home in
Berlin. He did so unwillingly, both because he resented his continuing dependency on his father and because the tensions
between the latter and his wife were becoming more and more
obvious. In any case, he was also keeping open the option of an
academic career in law and/or history, by writing – under the
supervision of a great legal historian, Levin Goldschmidt – a
substantial monograph on early juridical forms of commercial
enterprise in late-medieval Italy (*The History of Commercial
Partnerships in the Middle Ages*, published in 1889). Following

the exacting requirements of a career in the prestigious German academic system, two years later he published a second scholarly work, *Roman Agrarian History and Its Significance for Public and Civil Law (Die Römische Agrargeschichte und ihre Bedeutung für das Staats und Privatrecht).*

Both these books indicate Weber's great interest in themes that lie between economic and legal history. They were successful enough, in the appropriate circles, to induce him to reconsider his earlier preference for a career as a lawyer in favour of an academic career, possibly in the fields of economic history or commercial law. In the meantime, however, Weber's commitment to scholarship had found a somewhat different expression. In 1888 he had become a member of the *Verein für Sozialpolitik*, an 'association for social policy', among whose members were many academics with an interest in contemporary public issues. Soon, without interrupting his other activities, Weber engaged himself in a large-scale survey on behalf of the Verein, dealing with the current economic and social conditions of the rural populations in the part of Prussia lying east of the River Elbe, in what is today Polish territory. Within barely a year, Weber's sustained work on this project yielded a massive volume (*The Condition of Rural Workers in East-of-the-Elbe Germany/Die Lage der Landarbeiter im ostelbischen Deutschland* (1892)), where the survey's empirical findings were painstakingly assembled and thoroughly analysed.

The book gives evidence not only of its author's outstanding talent and energy, but also of the significance for him of two themes relevant to his later work. On the one hand, it expresses a concern regarding a trend that was apparent from the data: German rural workers were slowly abandoning the region and being progressively replaced by Polish workers, whom Weber does not hesitate to characterize as culturally inferior, and who in any case, as foreigners, constitute for the region a politically dangerous presence. On the other hand, it argues that those German workers who left the countryside were often motivated by interests transcending narrowly utilitarian and material ones, which 'homo oeconomicus' supposedly pursues to the exclusion of all others. They were seeking, at some cost to their economic security and that of their families, a degree of personal autonomy denied them by the patriarchal relations characteristic of the Junker estates.

The beginnings of Weber's academic career

Together with publications produced by another research project on a similar topic, in which Weber became involved in the same years at the behest of a Protestant association interested in promoting the welfare of the German working classes, Weber's published survey (mentioned above) played an unforeseen role in his career. Its survey of the rural workers on the eastern side of the Elbe, besides indicating the great intellectual energy of its author, suggested that this young scholar, though trained chiefly as a jurist and a historian of economics and law, could also be considered an economist. In any case, the book seems to have played a significant role in the otherwise baffling fact that an important German university, that of Freiburg, offered its chair of economics to Weber. (The German expression *Volkswirtschaft* literally means 'national economy'). Although he was also being considered for appointment in the law faculty at the University of Berlin at that time, he accepted the 'call' from Freiburg in 1893, in spite of his awareness that he was not qualified as an expert in the discipline he was to profess.

This early success (Weber was less than thirty years old at the time) secured for him the economic independence from his family he had long aspired to. It also allowed him to marry his fiancée, Marianne Ange Schnitger, a young relative on his father's side. The couple was destined to remain childless and, according to some sources, the life which Max and Marianne shared did not have a serious sexual dimension.

From other standpoints, however, the Webers formed a very close couple, especially in comparison with that constituted by Max Senior and Helene. By now, Max Weber felt much closer to his mother than to his father, and his preference was shared by Marianne, who was always on very good terms with her mother-in-law. She was, on her own account, a scholar of considerable stature, but utterly committed to placing her whole existence at the service of her husband and his career.

In 1895, in his belated inaugural lecture at Freiburg, Weber emphatically proclaimed his own nationalistic ideals. In their name, he criticized the German bourgeoisie for its unwillingness to face up to the political responsibilities of a ruling class, or to step openly into the public sphere in order to modernize the country's political and administrative institutions. In the same spirit, he proposed an expressly non-technical, highly political definition of the tasks of the discipline he was professing at Freiburg.

In the following year, however, Weber accepted a call from a more important university, that of Heidelberg, where he had studied previously, and moved there as, again, professor of economics. As he had done in Freiburg, in Heidelberg too Weber threw himself with great energy into academic work, and established close, though sometimes difficult, contacts with distinguished students of other disciplines – for instance, the theologian Troeltsch and the jurist Jellinek.

He also continued to take an interest in public affairs by conducting research on current issues – in particular, on the operations of the German stock market. At one point he also considered, but did not pursue, the possibility of becoming a candidate for election to the Reichstag, the legislative body of the German empire.

A serious crisis and the comeback from it

The year 1897 was a dramatic one for Max Weber and his wife Marianne. They invited to stay with them, in a newly bought house in Heidelberg, Max's mother, Helene, to whom he and Marianne had become increasingly attached. But Max Senior insisted on accompanying his wife to Heidelberg, and during his stay there his behaviour towards her became more and more objectionable. This led to a serious altercation between him and his son, who was now his host, and who in this capacity asked his own father to leave his house. Within a few weeks, Max Weber Senior suddenly died.

Soon after this, a lengthy period of acute psychological distress began for the younger Max, who endured a sequence of sufferings, lasting for many years, with only occasional improvements and intermissions. Eventually, this condition made it impossible for Weber to practise his vocation as a professor effectively, and he was unable to continue the intense programme of research and publication which he had been conducting successfully for years. The symptoms of this condition, writes a commentator, were physical tiredness, insomnia, internal tension, guilt feelings, anxiety attacks and unceasing agitation. As Marianne was to write in her biography of her husband, 'everything had become too much for him; he was no longer able to read, to write, to talk, to walk or sleep without torment'. As a scholar in his thirties, who had already given evidence of outstanding talent in diverse fields, Weber now found himself suddenly and inexplicably unable to pursue his passion for teaching and research; he could neither structure nor publicly justify his very existence.

In the period between 1897 and 1903, Weber tried intermittently to restart himself on his work, including teaching, or to undergo treatment: but for years these attempts had only limited and temporary success. To moderate, at least occasionally, the profound sense of embarrassment and guilt which this situation engendered, Weber, either by himself or with his wife, made repeated trips, particularly to Italy, a country they both liked very much. He also persistently tried to modify the terms of his contract with the University of Heidelberg, in view of the fact that he was no longer able to hold courses or seminars.

There were repeated highs and lows in this condition until, in 1903, Weber, while remaining psychologically unfit to resume teaching, found himself again able to read systematically, to conduct research and to publish. He even decided to take over, with two other scholars, the editing of an important scientific journal, the *Archiv für Sozialwissenschaft und Sozialpolitik*. In the second half of 1904, he published an important methodological essay in this journal, which later formed the first part of his most famous study, *The Protestant Ethic and the Spirit of Capitalism*. This essay immediately found a relatively wide audience and aroused much controversy in the academic milieu, to which it also gave notice that Max Weber was in the saddle again. In the same year, the Webers travelled to the United States, and Max took part in a scholarly conference held in St Louis (Missouri) in the context of the World Exhibition; they also spent a few weeks in the country, meeting distant relatives and academic personalities.

In 1905 Weber's persistent attention to political affairs found new expression in the interest awakened in him by the Russian Revolution of that year. Within a few weeks, Weber, whose knowledge of languages included the classical and romance languages, as well as English and Hebrew, learned Russian well enough to be able to read documents and other sources in the language, and wrote long essays on the current developments in the Tsarist empire. In 1908 he took on the task of editing – for the editor Siebeck of Tübingen – an entirely new edition of a well-established but now outdated collective, multi-volume work on economic and related phenomena, which was to be entitled *Grundrisse der Sozialoekonomie* (*Outlines of Social Economics*). The following year, with Georg Simmel and Werner Sombart, Weber was one of the founding members of the German Sociological Association. He also remained involved in the activities of the *Verein für Sozialpolitik*, where for years he contested the current leadership, largely composed of older scholars of a conservative political, social and intellectual orientation.

Weber had a tendency to become passionately interested, and occasionally involved, in causes that were distinctly unpopular in his social milieu, such as feminism and the right of socialist students and women to have access to university studies and academic professions. He also tended to criticize openly and sharply those views with which he dissented, in particular racism and anti-Semitism, very common in German academic circles. This willingness to engage himself on behalf of various controversial causes is one of the attractive characteristics of Weber's personality, but sometimes embroiled him in serious quarrels, and on a couple of occasions even led him to consider challenging his opponents and detractors to duels.

In the years immediately preceding the First World War, Weber engaged actively, single-handed, in a large and demanding research project: a series of comparative-historical essays dealing with the most significant religions that had developed throughout the centuries, in Palestine, in India, in China, in the West and in the Arab world. We have already mentioned a further, absorbing task – the general editorship of the *Grundrisse* project, to which he intended to contribute a volume on the general theme of the broader social context of economic phenomena. Over the years, this contribution increasingly took the form of a wide-ranging sociological treatise, dealing not only with those phenomena, but also with juridical, political and religious ones, again from a comparative-historical perspective.

The Great War

The start of what was to be called the First World War, and in particular the strategic and diplomatic conditions under which the German empire undertook it, confirmed the validity of criticisms that Weber had long voiced, publicly or privately, against his own country's policies and its leadership (or lack of it, as he saw the matter). In spite of this, Weber responded to the beginning of the war itself with the passion of a true patriot. He presented himself for military service, but, given his health conditions and his age, he was able to take on only an administrative role, with the rank of captain, in the management of a military hospital in Heidelberg; and in 1915 he found himself compelled to resign even this responsibility. He continued to work hard at his scholarly projects over the next few years, during which he also engaged in intense public activities, chiefly by commenting on ongoing political affairs in prestigious national papers.

In 1917 this activity culminated in a series of articles on the changes which, according to Max Weber, would have to be made in the constitution of the Reich, and particularly in the relationship between government and parliament assuming that Germany and its ally Austria won the war (as he continued to hope). Essentially it was a matter of constitutionalizing the political arrangements of the country (beginning with those of its dominant component, Prussia) much more seriously than its leadership had so far allowed. In response to the sacrifices the masses had made during the war, the political process would have to be democratized.

In these articles, understandably, Weber did not consider the possibility of the Reich's military defeat of the Reich, though he may have foreseen this, given the pessimism he sometimes expressed about the way the German High Command conducted not only military, but also economic, political and diplomatic affairs. It is possible that he did not openly profess all his misgivings because of the censorship the Command was practising.

In any case, at the end of 1918 the Reich's defeat, and the inglorious end of the long historical career of the Hohenzollern dynasty (Wilhelm II abdicated both as King of Prussia and as Emperor) caused Weber profound dismay, and gave a tragic cast to what remained of his life. Nevertheless, he took a realistic attitude towards the German republic. Whatever the rights and wrongs of its hasty proclamation, and the weaknesses of its improvised leadership, Weber – unlike many academic colleagues and members of the bourgeoisie – recognized the legitimacy of the new regime and was willing to cooperate with its leaders in confronting the country's disastrous situation.

He took part with other experts in the discussion over the republic's constitution (the so-called Weimar Constitution), and in the process of doing so he attacked views that were prevalent both on the right and on the left of the new political system. He took part in the negotiations of the Peace Treaty at Versailles, and opposed the vindictive economic reparations and the humiliating political conditions the victorious Western powers were imposing on defeated Germany. As a member of the German Democratic Party, Weber took an active part in public debates, but had no success when it came to standing for election.

In the course of 1918, however, Weber also found it possible to undertake academic activities from which he had excluded himself for two decades. That year, he accepted a chair at the University of Vienna, and successfully (though with great effort) taught courses there, but in 1919 was invited to the University of Munich. Here again he committed himself intensely to teaching, without giving up either his activity as commentator on political affairs, or his commitment to two large research projects: editing the new edition of *Outlines of Social Economics* (to which he contributed *Economy and Society*); and the comparative studies on 'the ethic of the world religions' (Parsons (ed.) 1930; Gerth and Mills (eds) 1946; Gerth (ed.) 1951; Gerth and Martindale (eds) 1952, 1958).

In 1920, both these projects bore fruit in successful publications. One is the first volume of a three-volume set, containing revised editions of the comparative-historical essays on world religions, which had so far appeared in several issues of the *Archiv*. This volume also contains a general introduction, and a new edition of *The Protestant Ethic* and of a related essay, *The Protestant Sects and the Spirit of Capitalism*. Weber also prepared for publication a first volume of his contribution to the *Grundrisse der Sozialoekonomie*, on which he had been working for many years. However, on 14 June 1920, in Munich, Weber died of pneumonia, without having been able to complete either of these two scholarly undertakings. In the following years his widow, Marianne, devoted much effort to the posthumous publication of volumes containing Weber's essays, and to the edition of the scholarly materials he had prepared over many years for *Economy and Society*. She also wrote a massive, well-documented biography of her husband.

What kind of a man was Max Weber?

From Marianne Weber's biography and from later ones, all of them to a greater or lesser extent indebted to Marianne's, one can derive some elements of an answer to this question.

Undoubtedly, Max Weber had a number of appealing human traits. He was known, for instance, to be prone to frequent and loud laughter. Even while he was unable to fully practise his profession, his wife's talents as a hostess allowed him to gather round himself a circle of colleagues and students, which met frequently at the Webers' and which all parties found most stimulating and satisfying. As we saw, he would become passionately involved in various cultural and social causes, including controversial ones. These, and his incredible capacity for work (aside from the awful parenthesis of the nervous breakdown) are very significant, positive aspects of his personality.

One must set over this, however, the fact that Weber was a tormented man, for he experienced conflicting passions with equal intensity. He was first and foremost a scholar, engaged in a strenuous effort to learn, understand, interpret, and produce and convey new knowledge in diverse fields. But during some phases of his existence, as we have seen, he was compelled to suspend that effort, and for a while he must have suspected that he would never again be capable of it.

Furthermore, Weber's conception of the role of a scholar, and particularly of a social scientist, committed him to limiting as far as possible the interference of his own values – held with passionate intensity – with his scholarly activity. His personal moral commitments, and his political preferences, were not allowed to affect the results of his studies, for this would limit or negate their objectivity – a value which he thought all scholars should pursue.

At the same time, Weber was well aware that this attempt to separate his own values from his work as a scholar was by its nature difficult to achieve. Also, he held that a person committed exclusively to scholarship would deprive his very existence of moral significance. Such a person would become an uprooted and bloodless individual, which Weber himself definitely did not want to be.

But what other identity could provide a balance to, and complement, his identity as a scholar? Weber thought that there was an inevitable tension between the values to which a person can commit himself in order to confer some significance to his own existence, and this was particularly the case for the values central, respectively, to religious experience, erotic experience, economic activity, aesthetic creation and enjoyment, politics and science. Whoever wants to commit their existence to some of these values must necessarily turn their back on the other ones.

Weber once wrote of himself that he felt 'unmusical' from the religious standpoint, suggesting that religious concerns did not evoke a strong personal response in him. So far as we know, until fairly late in life (when he had one, or perhaps two, serious extramarital relations) he was not involved in any intense erotic experience. From a material viewpoint, he held a privileged social position, both as a university professor and as a member of a well-to-do family, which protected him from the necessity of working for profit. Finally, some of his critics claim that he had a limited aesthetic sensitivity.

Given this, the only set of values which counted for him, besides those appropriate to scholarship, were those appropriate to the political sphere. But whoever has a strong interest in politics – whether 'high' or 'low' politics, pertaining respectively to the competition for power between sovereign states in the international arena or to *who gets what* in domestic affairs – must perforce be a partisan, for he must wish his country or his party to attain and maintain a position of advantage over all others, and if possible work to that effect.

By the same token, he cannot afford to be objective in forming his judgements and in committing his energy and his passion (*right or wrong, my country*). Thus, he must reject, or at any rate distance himself from, the concern with impartiality and objectivity that is characteristic of the scholar.

Weber's political passion could at times overrun the restraint represented by his professional values as a scholar. His Freiburg inaugural lecture aroused much comment because it contained many affirmations of his nationalist fervour; and his judgements on political personalities of his time could at times be unfairly sharp and dismissive. Yet he never had an opportunity to express that passion by performing a responsible role in contemporary politics, or by making a difference to the policies of the German empire and later of the German republic. He was not able to *matter*, in politics, except in the capacity of an observer, a commentator or a critic. He was denied any opportunity to present and justify himself in political contests or to take policy initiatives and bear the related risks, in the capacity of a statesman or a politician. His penetrating, far-seeing judgement on political affairs (international and domestic) often convinced those close to him that he had the makings of a true statesman; but it was never matched by an effective capacity for Weber to assert himself as a protagonist on the political scene.

Thus, while Weber was tormented by the contrast between the two chief spheres of his own existence, scholarship and partisanship, he was also frustrated by the fact that he could not personally work to attain the interests to which he attributed the highest significance – the security and the might of the German nation. Furthermore, he suffered a similar frustration in his identity as a scholar, during the years when all his professional activity was nearly paralysed, and subsequently, since it was many more years before he was able even to teach again.

On all these accounts, one can well understand why the biographers of Max Weber, beginning with his wife, very often label Weber's character 'vulcanic'. His existence appears marked by a deep and tragic internal tension, which found its most open expression in the breakdown, but for some years before and after that frequently manifested itself in various other psychosomatic symptoms.

Weber's scholarly legacy

Fortunately for posterity, during that tormented and relatively brief existence (he died at fifty-six) Weber produced an imposing scholarly *oeuvre*, on which rests the current standing of his name. A recent book on Weber lists over two hundred writings (though some of them appear more than once, corresponding to different editions). The great majority of these, of course, refer not to books but to essays, reviews or occasional writings of various nature and size.

Weber himself, shortly before his death, decided to collect into a set of three volumes the essays on the sociology of religion. After his death, other writings of his were published in collections edited by his wife or by other scholars. Mostly, the secondary literature on Weber makes reference chiefly to these works, many of which have appeared also in more or less complete and correct translations in other languages, including English. To remedy gaps or other flaws of those collections, in the 1980s German scholars initiated the publication of a complete edition of Weber's works – the *Max Weber Gesamtausgabe*. This monumental publishing effort has already yielded several impressively produced volumes, but is not yet complete. Once it is, it will comprise a few dozen volumes, divided into three sections: *Writings and Speeches*, *Letters* and *Lectures*.

The preparation of the *Gesamtausgabe* has variously improved on the ways in which previous editions had presented Weber's writings, and offers a better basis for the reconstruction of his biography and of his thought. But it has proceeded somewhat haltingly (some volumes are currently many years behind the publication date originally planned), and in many cases the sophisticated and painstaking editorial work that has gone into it has only marginally modified the results previously achieved by two earlier generations of editors.

The bulk of Weber's scholarly legacy can be grouped into six clusters of texts, each characterized by one basic theme. The published English translations of the most significant writings within each cluster are in the select bibliography at the end of this book.

1   Writings on economic history.
2   Writings analysing the findings of empirical research projects conducted by Weber on east-of-the-Elbe rural workers, and on the German stock market, and on industrial work conditions.
3   Writings on the nature of the cultural sciences and on their methodology.
4   Writings on the sociology of religion: the most significant among these are book-length essays which discuss, in sequence, Calvinism, Confucianism and Taoism, Hinduism and Buddhism, and ancient Judaism (Parsons (ed.) 1930; Gerth and Mills (eds) 1946; Gerth (ed.) 1951; Gerth and Martindale (eds) 1952, 1958). Others, of lesser dimensions but sometimes of great significance, discuss more than one religion in a comparative framework. All these writings were originally collected in the *Gesammelte Aufsätze zur Religionssoziologie* but are or will be edited separately in the *Gesamtausgabe*. One must also mention in this context a lengthy section of *Economy and Society* which deals with the sociology of religion.
5   Writings on general sociology and on the relationship between economic phenomena on the one hand and religious, juridical and political phenomena on the other: the most important of such writings are part of *Economy and Society*, edited, first, by Marianne Weber after the First World War, and then by Johannes Winckelmann after the Second World War.
6   Finally, political writings: some of these were occasioned by contemporary developments; others are of a more scholarly nature.

This book will take into account almost exclusively the writings that fall in the groupings 3 to 6 (but not *all* such writings!). The main concern is to present Weber's theoretical positions regarding the nature of the socio-historical process in general and the genesis and nature of modern society in particular. But before we approach these topics we have to ask ourselves how Weber conceived the actual task of a science of social phenomena.

2
Questions of Method

The German controversy on the method of the cultural sciences

Wilhelmine Germany had an outstanding system of higher education, arguably the best in the world. Teaching and research were conducted to very high standards both in the natural sciences, such as physics, chemistry and physiology, and in other disciplines, such as law, theology, history and philology. These are characterized by their concern with phenomena that differ from natural ones because they are generated by human agency and because they constrain and orient human conduct. A generic term for these disciplines, which qualifies them as scientific – the German expression *Wissenschaft* has a broader scope than the English expression 'science' – is *Kulturwissenschaften*, sciences of culture. (Another such expression is *Geisteswissenschaften*, literally 'sciences of the spirit' or 'of the mind'.) Taken as a whole, these were juxtaposed with the sciences of nature, the *Naturwissenschaften*, as equally legitimate components of the scientific enterprise.

But this juxtaposition was not unproblematical. In the course of the Wilhelmine era, an intense and prolonged intellectual debate took place in Germany regarding both the epistemological status of, and the appropriate methodology for, the *Kulturwissenschaften*, and their differences and particularities with respect to the *Naturwissenschaften*.

The natural sciences aim to produce empirically grounded generalizations that are valid for whole classes of natural phenomena, laws which account for them and technical instruments to control their occurrence. By fulfilling such objectives, these sciences have yielded remarkable intellectual and practical results. For this reason some practitioners of the *Kulturwissenschaften* have argued that their disciplines should, as much as possible, take the natural sciences as a model and reproduce or approximate their strategies of research. Thus, they should accord great significance to the collection of empirical data through the systematic observation of phenomena, the discovery of regularities and the formation of generalizations from such data, the search for causal relationships between variables, the testing of such relationships through experiments and so on.

This project (which we may label positivistic) was even more strongly advanced in France and in England than in Germany. However, this led many German practitioners of the *Kulturwissenschaften* to hold that project in suspicion and often to reject it outright. They aligned themselves with those intellectuals who emphasized the political, moral and cultural differences between Germany and the rest of Europe, projecting themselves as the custodians of a distinctive, superior version of the European spirit, loftier and nobler because not tainted by the suspect inheritance of the Enlightenment and by contemporary positivism. This version was characterized by a great respect for the past, an attachment to 'culture' as against 'civilization' and a commitment to the values of moral experience – of aesthetic enjoyment and of philosophical contemplation. It placed less significance, within scholarly activity, on the possibility of treating cultural phenomena scientifically and of controlling them practically. Such phenomena, they insisted, are intrinsically historical, for, unlike natural phenomena, they differ significantly according to where, how and when they take place.

This conception of the professional activity of students of the cultural sciences was not exclusive to German practitioners but was articulated by them with particular emphasis. It devalued and condemned the ways in which other students defined the objectives and the strategies of research of those sciences.

According to such a conception, for instance, German scholars should not attempt to construct a science of economic phenomena in the way in which this was being done in Great Britain or in Austria. Here, economic phenomena were treated chiefly by means of deductive reasoning, starting from a human agent construed exclusively as 'homo oeconomicus'. This abstract, 'one-dimensional' entity sought to maximize its own utility in a self-consciously egoistic, narrowly rational manner, indifferent to the particularities of specific historical situations, to varying institutional environments or to value considerations, to the moral boundaries which these impose upon human action. The 'historical school' of economics long dominant in Germany sought, instead, to build a science of economic phenomena inductively, accumulating empirical data from existing records, then reconstructing the material and institutional constraints on economic activity, together with its outcomes in different countries at different times. It aimed to establish and emphasize the national particularities of economic development, and to understand the orientation which actors (particularly collective actors) gave their own economic activities in different locales and different phases of history.

In the same manner, the attempt which Comte had made in France to comprehend the whole story of the human species as a sequence, with three successives phases, was considered in Germany to be extremely superficial and misleading. A similar condemnation was directed at the intellectual legacy of Marxism, represented in Wilhelmine Germany by Friedrich Engels and by other intellectuals of the so-called Second International. That legacy was also criticized for failing to recognize the significance of such phenomena as religion, law and politics, for promoting class warfare, and for underestimating the significance of national commonalities and of the power struggle among sovereign states.

This radical refusal to model the scope and method of the cultural sciences upon those of the natural sciences, however, was not universally shared by the German practitioners of the former sciences. According to some of them, that refusal, at any rate in its more radical expressions, had unacceptable implications, and threatened to compromise the project itself of a *science* of cultural phenomena. For one thing, it authorized scholars to rely upon their own intuitive evaluation of the nature and significance of the facts relating to a given topic of research, and on their capacity to communicate such intuitions persuasively, rather than to dispassionately analyse those facts in order to verify them.

In conducting their researches and expounding their findings, such scholars eschewed constructing and employing concepts of a more general scope, which would have permitted and required systematic comparisons between individual instances of certain phenomena. They asserted the exclusive significance, instead, of the particular circumstances of the events they studied, and of the unique course of those events. They discounted the possibility of *explaining* social phenomena, as against describing their course or interpreting their significance. They held that the formulations of statements about social facts could be legitimately influenced by the scholar's subjective preferences and particularly by their moral and political preferences, thus denying implicitly or explicitly that such statements could or should be objectively valid.

Positions of this kind also evoked dissent from scholars who recognized the distinctiveness of socio-cultural as against natural phenomena, and who did not subscribe to the positivistic project of studying the former exactly like the latter. Such dissent led to a lively and prolonged intellectual debate (the so-called *Methodenstreit*, dispute on methods) within the intellectual community of students of the cultural sciences.

The dispute reflected, among other things, a keen philosophical concern, largely inspired by the legacy of Kant, with the conditions under which valid knowledge can be achieved in any field. But it also had significant political and social implications. On various occasions, Max Weber made very important contributions to this dispute, especially concerning a specific question – the role that value judgements could or should perform within the context of the cultural sciences. This chapter outlines some of those contributions, leaving aside others which I consider to be of lesser significance.

Weber's philosophical anthropology

To understand Max Weber's position on value judgements and allied matters, it is useful to refer to what could be called his philosophical anthropology, that is, his general understanding of the particularities of the human species. Among these the most significant particularity, which according to Weber should also determine the way humans understand and study themselves, is the following: human beings are on the one hand compelled, but on the other hand enabled, to locate themselves in the reality within which they exist (including the presence and the activity of other human beings), and to act within that reality, on the basis of the *meanings* they attribute to it.

It is not given to humans to live and act on the basis of a direct and full apprehension of reality itself, of all phenomena the one that impinges most directly on our existence. First, as Kant has taught us, reality as such is unknowable, except within the framework of subjective processes which select and order cognitively various phenomenal aspects of it. More generally, the reality within which human beings exist is too complex, ambiguous and threatening to enable them to orient not only cognitively but practically to that reality in its totality. They can only locate themselves and function within it by ordaining it subjectively, initially by attaching meaning to particular, selective aspects and moments of it. Such meaning, however, is not intrinsic to any given aspect, objectively built into it. It is unavoidably up to the human beings themselves to attribute such meaning, to interpret reality by considering some aspects and moments of it as central to their own existence, and others as peripheral or indifferent. It is up to them whether they value such aspects negatively or positively.

The process in question is intrinsically contradictory. On the one hand, it is unavoidably arbitrary, because it cannot refer to an uncontroversially, objectively given order within reality itself. On the other hand, if one recognizes the arbitrariness of the process, one runs the risk of depriving it of its intended effects. Acknowledging and emphasizing such arbitrariness would empty reality of significance, and would destabilize or relativize the ordering attributed to it by the meanings themselves. Human beings would be left prey to disorder, threatened by the sensation that in the end nothing is endowed with authentic significance.

In order to avoid this, the subjective attribution of significance to reality should not be recognized in its unavoidable arbitrariness. It must be experienced as the necessary recognition of meanings which are intrinsically given, and the dutiful acknowledgement of values which are intrinsically valid. In order to perform its task – to order reality – the subject's interpretation of reality cannot be seen as *just* any interpretation whatsoever, valid no more or less than any other one. Put otherwise, human beings by their nature *inscribe* meanings *on to* reality, but must delude themselves that *read* such meanings *off* reality.

The search for objectivity

This Weberian conception of the human being, which in Clifford Geertz's metaphor renders the human being similar to a spider hanging from a web which the spider itself weaves, has significant consequences, among other things, for the ways in which human beings understand and study themselves.

First, the process of attribution or imputation of significance, of meaning, is unavoidably a mental process, thus an individual process, for there are no minds other than those existing within and operating through the brain of a given member of the human species. Second, on this account the scientific understanding of human events, too, must ultimately refer directly or indirectly to mental processes, that is, to events and structures which are at bottom individual, having to do with the *actions* and *passions* of single individuals. It must take on board the ways in which these individuals interpret their own circumstances, and how they identify and assess the needs, the opportunities or the threats with which they are confronted in those circumstances. (This position was later labelled 'methodological individualism'.)

Put otherwise, the molecular aspect of that socio-historical reality which constitutes the domain of the sciences of culture is *action*. Action is individual behaviour which is specifically human because it is endowed with meaning, loaded with subjective significance and oriented by interpretive processes.

It is possible, in turn, to attain intellectually the action of somebody else – for practical or for scientific purposes – through a process which is itself interpretive: *Verstehen*, that is, 'understanding'.

However, this immediately raises a serious problem. Those who practise a science of culture are themselves human individuals. Their very activity is a complex sequence of actions, and thus of interpretive processes concerning the actions of others, searching to capture the interpretive processes of other individuals. Hence there is a danger: the interpretive operations of a student of human affairs, in so far as they reflect the values (the moral preferences, the general understandings of reality) to which the student herself has a personal orientation, may influence, to a greater or lesser extent, the way the student understands the events on which she bases the search. Those values may prevent her dispassionate ascertainment of the interpretive processes of other subjects by superimposing on them, in a more or less subconscious manner, the student's own evaluation of those processes and the relative behaviours.

Weber develops a complex position concerning this possibility. In the first place, according to him, the scientific nature of research on human phenomena is not necessarily threatened by the fact that, unlike the research of facts of nature, it involves subjective processes of interpretation and valuation. Paradoxically, according to Weber, research in the cultural sciences is in a position of advantage. Not only can it reconnoitre the external unfolding of certain events, but it can also attain an understanding of the motives, the intentions and the subjective processes which preside over that unfolding.

For instance, if we see a person brandishing a hatchet and chopping a tree trunk into logs, we may, beside describing this event in purely physical terms, interpret it and account for it by identifying the person's motivations. By chopping wood that person may prepare fuel for the winter, try to keep himself fit, or give expression to the anger aroused in him by the actions of a neighbour or a stranger, taking it out, as it were, on the tree trunk.

In the second place, there *is* a risk of a short circuit between the subjectivity of the researcher on the one hand and the subjectivity of the protagonists of the action under research, but it is not impossible to avoid or limit such risk. It is inevitable and it is appropriate that in deciding what to study the researcher should express her own value preferences – her own sense of the importance of a certain topic and of its relevance for problems to which she attaches subjective significance. But it is also possible for the student to limit this interference.

In conducting the research work itself, the student can (and, Weber argues, definitely ought to) strive to keep her own *value judgements* from biasing or determining her own *judgements of fact* concerning the phenomenon under research. To the extent that she manages to do this, she can expect other students of the same phenomenon, who do not share her value judgements, to assent to the validity of her own judgements of fact. In other words, if her research practice respects the radical difference (posited by Kant) between the two kinds of judgement – value judgements and judgements of fact – and she conducts her research correctly, the student can achieve objectively valid results.

What are the conditions of such objectivity? The condition is first the researcher's *Wertfreiheit* – a German expression sometimes misleadingly translated into English as 'value-freedom'. In his own research, that is, the researcher must give priority to ascertaining factual data, and keep his own preferences from interfering with or biasing that activity. A further condition is the observance of rules of intellectual honesty in ascertaining the facts, in particular the care taken in registering and classifying data, and the observance of logic in reasoning about the data themselves as well as their connections. (This principle, according to Weber, keeps the student from having recourse too easily to sheer *intuition*.) Finally, it is important that the student should employ in his own discourse clearly and expressly defined concepts, which characterize the different configurations a given social phenomenon assumes under different circumstances. Again these concepts must be 'non-evaluative', that is, must not contain value judgements.

Ideal types

This last point – the use of purposefully formed concepts as instruments whereby the student keeps at bay his own preferences and makes his own discourse 'value-free' – is an aspect of a further Weberian contribution concerning the methods of social research, that is, his theory of so-called 'ideal types'. Like other methodological positions taken by Weber, his understanding of ideal types also fights, so to speak, on two fronts.

On the one hand, Weber opposes those who overemphasize the peculiarity of the sciences of culture and their distance from natural sciences, by denying that the former can and should employ general concepts. Such students assert, for instance, that in the ancient political tradition of Germany the figure of the 'king' is characterized in a wholly particular manner. Germanic kingship, they maintain, is unique and therefore also irrepeatable, for instance in the way the king is selected, the nature and justification of his rule, the relationship he has with other powerful persons and the rest of the people. This, according to the argument, makes the Germanic king totally incomparable with the figure of the monarch as it appears, say, in French absolutism. Thus, the argument continues, it is pointless to entertain a general concept of kingship which overrides the differences between Germanic and French kings.

Weber considers this position contradictory, because if consistently followed it would require giving up the term of 'king' itself even when referring to the Germanic experience alone, for *it*, too, must have shown some variety in its historical development and in its different locales. That position, at base, would lead the student to turn her back, so to speak, on any concept at all, or indeed to language itself, for every linguistic expression necessarily embodies an understanding of that which all its referents have in common, if only to differentiate them from the referents of other expressions.

On the other hand, Weber also dissents from the opposite position, according to which there are not, or there should not be, any substantial differences between the concepts of the cultural sciences and those of the natural sciences. According to this position, too, the concepts of the cultural sciences should be attained inductively, by ascertaining and assembling, within a set of data considered as essentially equivalent one to the other, the traits common to all data. Instead, according to Weber, the concepts construed and employed by the cultural sciences necessarily have a different relationship to phenomena – a relationship which the expression 'ideal type' seeks to convey.

Here 'ideal' does not mean that such concepts indicate an optimal condition to which reality should tend. Rather, they characterize concrete events by considering them as empirical approximations to a set of traits which the student constructs in order to simplify the variations present in reality, in full awareness that none of those types fully and directly reproduces such variations.

To understand better this notion of 'ideal type' – which I confess to finding rather confusing – it may be useful to keep in mind that in many important writings (most particularly in *Economy and Society*), where Weber not only discusses the notion of ideal type but practises it, he does this not so much by constructing single ideal types as by constructing *typologies*, that is, ensembles, sets of ideal typical concepts. In doing so, I would suggest, he reveals the true intent of the notion of 'ideal type'.

To clarify such intent, I will start from a homely English proverb – 'there is more than one way of skinning a cat'. Without (of course!) referring to that proverb, Weber endorses the methodological injunction it entails for the students of social facts. That is, they should seek to capture in their research and to convey in their writings the variety which concrete historical reality always reveals, even when it addresses a single problem or theme. They should not consider such variety as irrelevant or insignificant, assuming or arguing, as it were, that there *is* only one way of skinning a cat. However, in order to construct or make use of typologies, students of social affairs should add a critical clause to that proverb, turning it into the following: 'there is more than one way of skinning a cat – but there are not *that many* ways!'

This enlarged version of the proverb commits such students to take into account two contrasting demands. On the one hand, they must as far as possible reflect in their work the infinite variety which concrete reality presents. On the other hand, they must convey such variety as economically as possible, by showing clearly and succinctly the fundamental alternatives which that variety itself reflects. *This* is what typologies are for: they convey variety but at the same time reveal the constraints upon it which reality itself reveals. They do so by purposefully constructing a small number of abstract configurations which, in spite of the variety of their concrete manifestations, socio-historical phenomena necessarily reveal.

In other words, every typology articulates and contrasts the basic solutions to which any given historical and cultural problem lends itself. The cognitive success of this operation is all the greater if and in so far as:

- the typology is composed of few types;
- each of these consists of a coherent set of traits which, so to speak, belong together, express the same fundamental inspiration; on this account:
- the types themselves differ markedly from one another; and finally:
- the types are constructed not in a purely ad hoc manner, but as alternative responses to a specific problem.

A fundamental typology

The nature of the problem varies a great deal between one and the other of Weber's several typologies. Among those presented in *Economy and Society* we find, in particular, an utterly general typology, applicable to *any* aspect or moment whatever of social experience. It looks at those which Weber considers as the sole fundamentally different responses to questions such as the following: How do people know how to act, in whatever circumstances? In how many significantly different ways can an individual orient his/her own action, whatever problem it addresses?

According to Weber, it is possible to answer this question in only four ways, all of which are abstract ways, coherently conceived and purposefully contrasted with one another, as required by the very nature of ideal types.

Human action can be oriented:

1 by tradition: that is, on the basis of the implicit or explicit assumption that what has been done in the past deserves and demands to be repeated in the present (and in the

future): in this case we can call it *traditional* action. But, instead, it can be oriented

2   by affect: here, the actor, instead of appealing to the past and assuming its validity as a guide for present action, behaves in ways suggested to him or imposed on him in the here and now by his unreflected feelings, his emotions: in which case we can call his action *affective*.

It may also be the case that the actor asks himself more or less explicitly which alternatives are open to him in the given circumstances, considering, what resources and obstacles the situation presents regarding his action. However, this more or less explicit consideration of the *means and ends* of action, which makes it *rational*, differs according to whether:

3   the actor chooses a course of action which reflects an absolute preference for a given end state, whose validity he takes for granted in all circumstances; or
4   he adopts whatever course of action has the greatest probability of success and the least cost.

We can label these last two orientations respectively as *value-rational* and *instrumentally rational*.

This is, as one can see, an extremely general typology. All the others that Weber constructs, in fact, are of lesser scope. They concern questions as different as the following two (for example): In what ways can a political entity provide for the economic costs of its own activity? In what ways, within a religious perspective, is it possible to reconcile the belief in a just, omniscient, omnipotent deity with the reality of evil – that is, with the fact that all too often concrete events (to use the words of the marquis de Sade) show us 'the happiness of vice and the unhappiness of virtue'?

Weberian typologies can serve either a generic end – to suggest how varied is the reality to which they refer, while at the the same time showing the boundaries upon such variations – or they can serve the more obvious, immediate end of selecting a given aspect of historical experience and assisting the student in enquiring into it.

Weber never suggested that 'ideal types' constitute a new, different and superior way, invented by him, of conceptualizing social reality. On the contrary, Weber talked about ideal types in order to clarify the ways in which many students before him had sought – more or less self-consciously – to describe, classify, understand and account for social facts.

Again, just two examples. One can consider as an ideal type the concept, mentioned above, of 'homo oeconomicus'. The same thing can be said of so-called 'historical materialism', that is, the Marxist thesis that the economic characteristics of a given society strongly condition the totality of its institutions and its ideological and cultural features. Both these conceptual constructions throw light on certain aspects and tendencies of reality, but are not exhaustive. The same thing can be said of other conceptual constructs, including those Weber himself produced in his own substantive work, and which (in my judgement) stand among his most significant contributions to modern social theory.

Sociology and history

Weber employed the notion of 'ideal type' in order to clarify the relationship between sociology and history. The latter was widely considered in his own time, on various counts, as the cultural science par excellence. History, like all other disciplines, social or natural, cannot do without concepts of more-or-less general reference. To employ a phrase from the Middle Ages: *de particularibus non est scientia*. But the construction of the concepts of which history avails itself is not, so to speak, its strong suit. By its nature, history emphasizes the uniqueness of the facts with which it deals, and privileges the details of events or the particularities of the causal sequences it enquires into.

For this very reason, the scientific activity of historians can and must be complemented and supported by that of scholars who commit themselves, instead, to the formation of appropriate bodies of concepts, that is of ideal types and typologies. These, as we have seen, identify constant or recurrent themes of historical action, particularly those of institution-building. They work out the fundamental alternatives which are constantly presented to the actors (individual and collective) engaged in such activities, despite variations in the details of their configurations in the here-and-now of specific historical situations.

This is the task which Max Weber, at any rate in some phases of his intellectual itinerary, assigns to sociology. He characterizes it, it has been said, as a 'handmaiden to history' – an intellectual endeavour which specializes in fashioning conceptual tool-boxes of which historians can avail themselves.

Understood in this way, the relations of ideal types with the reality studied by historians is open-ended. Because it is ideal, no type can fully reflect the empirical reality to which it refers. Concrete historical phenomena always straddle one or more ideal types, mix them and qualify one with aspects of others. Any historian who is interested in the particularities of the facts being studied will have to distance himself from any one ideal type. Furthermore, being instruments for research, and particularly for historical research, all ideal types can be continuously corrected, improved or replaced by others which can better assist the scholar.

Finally, in order to reflect the multiplicity and complexity of socio-historical reality, ideal types, or indeed typologies themselves, can be architectonically arranged. That is, every type within a given typology can be subdivided into two or more sub-types and each of these, perhaps, into two or more sub-sub-types.

For instance, Weber's great essay (or perhaps chapter – its position within his *oeuvre* is the subject of controversy) entitled *The City* posits an ideal-typical contrast between the Western and the Oriental city. Only in the West, according to his argument, are cities characterized by a certain physical size, a certain demographic density, and a degree of economic specialization and division of labour, together with a relatively high (though variable) degree of political and juridical autonomy with respect to the outlying territory. Furthermore, only here can one find a set of obligations and rights which constitute the status of 'citizenship'.

In the Oriental cities these features are lacking. This is, however, for different reasons in two chief sub-types: in the Chinese city, because the individuals making up a city's population continue to derive their identities from their village of origins and from membership in a kinship group; and in the

Indian city, because the caste system breaks up the city's population into groups which for ritual reasons are intent upon standing away from and excluding each other. Furthermore, as concerns the Western city itself, Weber variously constructs the sub-types represented: as the ancient city, the medieval city and the early-modern city. Also, he adds to these typifications others that relate to the geographical location and the economic base of different cities.

In *Economy and Society*, Weber follows the same procedure in a systematic manner. First, he locates a given problem and spells out its most general solutions. Then he takes one of these solutions and suggests that it can take different ideal-typical configurations. In addition, sometimes he shows a number of variants of each configuration.

At each successive level his argument becomes less abstract, approaching empirical reality without actually ever attaining it, for example, by showing in some detail, how, in sixteenth-century China, the emperor sought to ensure a degree of co-ordination between the activities of the mandarins – the functionaries assigned to given localities within the empire. However, typological discourse may also take the opposite direction, towards higher and higher levels of abstraction and generality, allowing the student to identify broader problems and a greater variety of alternative solutions. Furthermore, at each level, the argument can proceed in a comparative perspective, for each ideal type presupposes and sets boundaries for others: 'there is more than one way of skinning a cat!'

In my judgement, it is this ideal-typical discourse that gives the true measure of Weber's theoretical genius, of his unequalled capacity to conceptualize social phenomena. But the fact that it often results in a complex architecture of systematically arrayed sets of concepts and subconcepts has an unexpected consequence. It may lead the reader to think that Weber conducts a conceptual exercise as an end in itself, or even to suspect that Weber *enjoyed* fashioning more and more specific problems with more and more detailed solutions – that he practised and enjoyed the construction of ideal types as a kind of intellectual game.

This was not the case. Weber's typologies are always in a twofold relationship with historical reality: they originate from it and are intended to return to it. In the first place, his constructions are grounded in a huge store of historical knowledge, of universal scope, in some cases acquired by Weber through first-hand research, and in others from knowledge provided by the existing specialist literature. For example, on the basis of his study of the primary and secondary sources available regarding the political-administrative institutions of Imperial China, Weber conceptualized the devices for coordinating from the centre the activity of officials working in the periphery. In the second place, according to Weber, types and typologies must in turn justify themselves as instruments for further historical research.

This characterization of sociology as the 'handmaiden' to history, specializing in the construction of ideal-type concepts, reveals considerable intellectual ambitions in Weber's understanding of sociology (even though, in Wilhelmine Germany, it was not a particularly recognized discipline). In particular, as Weber conceives and practises it, this discipline transcends the contrast which other students considered unavoidable between, on the one hand, the project of *comprehending* historical phenomena, of interpreting them by referring to the intentions and motivations of individual actors (in turn, directly or indirectly grounded in interpretations of reality), and, on the other hand, the attempt to *explain* such phenomena.

Here, again, Weber's position is an alternative to two contrasting conceptions. He denies that it is impossible to reconcile these two scientific projects. For him, the task of sociology is that of *explaining by interpreting*. But he excludes the possibility of deriving explanations of cultural phenomena from universal laws governing human events, which can be identified and stated in general terms. His ideal types are not laws of this kind. At best, as in the case of historical materialism, they can be considered as hypotheses. As such, they can be used to account for certain events or certain tendencies in socio-historical reality: but one must be able to transcend them once they reach their cognitive limits. They should not be considered as absolutely valid and used as *passe-partouts*. This is due to the necessary selective – and thus in a sense arbitrary – character of every conceptual instrument, and of every argument which employs such instruments in a more or less self-conscious manner.

As a result, within intellectual and scientific discourse, though not perhaps in the realm of cosmic intuition or aesthetic expression, it is not possible to attain the totality of phenomena or to attribute to such phenomena a meaning different from those attributed to them by individual subjects, nor is it possible to identify the necessary destination of the unfolding of socio-historical processes.

Social reality is intrinsically contingent, and its future open-ended. The most its student can do is to locate, hypothetically and provisionally, certain regularities of past development and certain tendencies of current development, without considering the former as utterly determined or the latter as ineluctable. Furthermore, by referring again to sets of ideal concepts, the student can become aware of and convey both the element of contingency in events ('there is more than one way of skinning a cat') and the element of necessity ('but there are not that many ways!'). In doing so, the student differentiates herself both from those who claim that historical events are intrinsically unpredictable and not subject to identifiable causal processes, and from those who consider it as totally determined, and believe, like Marx, that the whole course of human history constitutes a single riddle and that there is a definitive and universal solution to this riddle (in the case of Marx, through communism).

Social science and social practice

This conception of research on socio-historical phenomena, and of sociology in particular, is remarkably ambitious, but involves a fairly restrictive view of the relationship between social science and social practice. As we have seen, the student, in order to give an objective status to an enquiry which inevitably refers to the interpretive activity of individuals, must in turn set boundaries on his own interpretive activity. He must keep his own value judgements from short-circuiting the search for objectivity. He must also, in his researches, refer to sets of ideal-typical concepts, that are as comprehensive as possible and systematically worked out. But this implies that the student of social affairs, *qua* student, is not in a position to tell others (or even himself?) what to do or how to act.

If a political actor asks for advice on what policies to pursue, the most that even a student of politics can do, in that capacity, is to indicate the alternative courses of action in given circumstances, the necessary conditions for the success of each alternative, the ways in which the actor ought to act in order to attain such success and the probable consequences. He may, in particular, point out the possible negative impact of such consequences on values different from those on which the political actor's own choices are based (as well as, perversely, the sometimes negative effects of those consequences on the actor's own values). In other words, the student can clarify to the politician the connections between his ends and the means at his disposal – but cannot and should not determine the ends themselves, which the politician must determine on his own account, and pursue on his own responsibility.

The same self-denying ordinance is appropriate to the relationship between the scholar and those who turn to him for help in determining the meaning of their own existence, and the moral rules by which to orient themselves. It is not possible to give scientifically valid answers to such requests. Each individual must confront these questions on his own, on the basis of his own values, even if these values are in turn derived from his social and religious memberships. It is even more necessary for the student to set such boundaries on his own conduct when his professional role is that of a teacher and his own students ask him for moral advice, motivated by the authority vested within the teacher's role, which is increased by the cultural and social prestige of science.

These limitations are imposed on himself by the scholar *qua* scholar, in particular when as a teacher he speaks in the classroom from the lectern, for this position in principle protects him from criticism and from a systematic confrontation with alternative positions. By the same token, those limitations do not apply to the scholar when he presents himself and acts as a citizen, as a publicist, as a partisan or as a moral being who makes his own personal choices and, without appealing to the authority of science, tries to communicate them to others and to convince others of the validity of those choices.

In fact, according to Weber, a scholar who seeks to be *just* a scholar in all the phases and aspects of her existence, runs the risk of losing or weakening her moral nerve and finally her own humanity, for in so doing she denies herself a fervent and passionate commitment to particular ideals and values (and all ideals and values can only be particular), and the related experience of moral responsibility. And this experience, according to Weber, is necessary to *any* individual seeking to impart meaning to his/her own existence.

3
Weber's Conception of the Socio-Historical Process

An individualistic perspective on collective action

A significant American book on Max Weber synthesizes as follows some of the arguments that were briefly discussed in the last chapter:

> an emotion-laden debate . . . raged among historians in Weber's time. This debate concerned the adequacy of a historiography that focuses on individual actions, events, and persons, and treats the state as the center of all historical dynamics.
>
> Weber's conception of sociology acquires an obvious sense and identity when interpreted as a reaction to the continued intellectual and institutional hegemony of German historicist political historiography preoccupied with individual events and actions of decision makers . . . [B]ehind Weber's methodological elaborations concerning the ideal type stands the conviction that historiography must not limit its concerns to individual occurrences and actions but must pay attention to the impact of 'structural' forces and 'collective' phenomena on the course of historical developments. Weber's sociology, accordingly, appears above all as an attempt to conceptualize, *on the basis of a methodological individualism*, the structural and collective aspects of historical reality that were neglected by the guardians of the institutionalized historiographical tradition. (Burger 1987: x; emphasis added)

In this extract I have emphasized the clause 'on the basis of a methodological individualism' because it points out the main difficulty of the task at hand. How is it possible, on *that* basis, to attain an interpretation of historical events, and more generally of social reality, which takes into account its structural and collective aspects?

Weber's commitment to methodological individualism distances him from the attempts made by various authors, in Germany as elsewhere, to impute social events to the motions of something like a 'group mind', of which individual minds are merely a refraction. It also excludes a view of society as a unitary, organic whole, a self-standing entity which lies as it were on top of individuals, and controls and manages their activities. From that viewpoint, those activities, and those of the groups they make up, would be perceived as constituting the performance, self-aware or not, of tasks assigned them by the needs of the social whole. The category of 'function' would replace that of 'action'.

But, as we have seen, Weber anchors to action his own view of society. Such action, understood as activity endowed with meaning, reflects a considered perception of what is and what ought to be, and is necessarily individual. It engages the energies, the intentions, the preferences and the choices of individuals – though, naturally, of individuals situated in contexts. But, as in Sartre (*l'enfer, c'est les autres*), a basic component of those contexts is constituted by other individuals, each in turn capable of action.

This entails contrasting consequences. On the one hand, the possibility of inter-individual conflict arises if the individuals within a group have incompatible views, preferences or projects. And indeed, for Weber, conflict is always possible (at any rate latently) in the relations between individuals (and groups). It may happen, in particular, that a given individual views others as obstacles to the attainment of his own ends, or even seeks to treat others as means to that attainment. Hence the abiding possibility of a contrast over *who*, when all is said and done, manages to get rid of or to instrumentalize *whom*.

On the other hand, it may happen that the minds of some individuals harbour judgements, preferences and values that are compatible with, or even closely similar to, those harboured in the minds of others. At the very least, such compatibility would allow them to work in the presence of others without conflict. Further, a close similarity may induce all those individuals to align the respective lines of action with one another, to pool their energies and resources, to pursue shared projects, and to build and manage jointly within contexts that are accepted and appreciated by all.

Weber does not consider this second situation as necessarily more significant than the first. To orient oneself to the hostility of others is as much constitutive of action as it is to orient oneself to their benevolence or their neutrality. Both, in fact, turn action into *social* action – action, that is, undertaken by individuals in the light not only of their own subjective processes but also of those which they acknowledge in, or impute to, others. Furthermore, a non-conflictual situation is often the result of the resolution of a previous, conflictual one. But such a result is provisional and potentially unstable, for its persistence is threatened by the possibility that the previous conflict flares up again, or a new one takes its place. In addition, even when certain subjects share some perspectives and preferences and commit themselves to joint activity on behalf of these, very often they do so due to their conflict with others who pursue contrasting interests.

The genesis of collective actors

In Weber's view, then, groups develop when a plurality of individuals, each oriented in conduct by subjective processes of his/her own, is, as it were, traversed by commonalities existing between the respective processes. These groups develop if and to the extent that all individuals share values, judgements and preferences. Groups thus constituted are, for Weber, the true protagonists of the socio-historical process. Sometimes Weber designates them with the expression *Stände*. This is the plural form of *Stand*, a word which in other contexts means social rank, estate or status group. Its more generic meaning, however, points to any plurality of individuals emerging from the sharing of certain interests and capable of acting collectively towards them.

Which interests? The most diverse ones. It is well known that Weber characterized this diversity in the phrase 'material and ideal interests'. Note that here the noun 'interest' may seem an echo of Marx's conception of the historical process, where protagonists are groups (generally: classes) that conflict with one another in the pursuit of antagonistic economic interests. But Weber's adjectival couple 'material/ ideal' contradicts the Marxist view which privileges one, distinctly material, aspect of social existence by relating only the interests in play to it, and which assigns a derivative and secondary role to different interests. By the same token, the material/ideal view denies such privilege to purely ideal aspects of social existence.

Weber's awareness of social diversity is echoed in his multiple references to the distinction by the German sociologist Ferdinand Tönnies between *Gemeinschaft* ('comunity') and *Gesellschaft* ('association', 'society'). This emphasizes not only the diversity of interests that can be shared and jointly pursued, but also the diversity arising from ways in which individuals relate to one another and structure the groupings they form in the pursuit of those interests.

So far, we have considered one implication of the fact that all individual action takes place within contexts characterized by a plurality of individuals capable of action. On that account individuals may ally themselves or conflict with others. Both alternatives matter, historically, not so much at the level of the single individual, but in terms of the *Stände* they jointly constitute. Each *Stand* is held together by some lines of action which are shared within it; but in seeking to assert its interests (material or ideal) it typically encounters other *Stände* and possibly clashes with them.

The outcomes of such encounters shape the contexts within which confrontations between the *Stände* continue. Typically, one *Stand* prevails on the other to the extent that it can induce it to accept the priority of its own interests. Again, these can be material (relating, for instance, to arrangements for producing and distributing wealth, and in particular to the possession or exclusion from possession of the related resources) or ideal (relating, for instance, to the ways in which the cosmos and the afterlife are conceived, and to the appropriate practices for obtaining the good will of the deity and securing salvation).

Power and its forms

If a context within which various *Stände* coexist is characterized by the privilege one of them has of asserting its own superiority over the others, and thus conditioning their existence, one can expect such a privilege to be a prime object for contention. On what, then, does a given *Stand*'s ability depend, in order to secure that privilege, while denying it to others?

Weber's answer to this question appears simple and formal at first: it depends on the power relations between the *Stände*. This is a less obvious and anodyne answer than it may seem, for different ones have been given in the history of social thought. For instance, in the Hegelian dialectical tradition, to which Marx belongs in this regard, at critical junctures in history a group's ability to assert itself over others depends on its greater disposition to realize a universal interest. (In Marx, this lies in the creation of ever more effective productive arrangements, which themselves reflect humanity's ever-growing capacity to control nature by means of technology.)

But this, and other conceptions of history as progress, where a group's success reveals and celebrates its objective merits and the intrinsic superiority of its values, are foreign to Weber's thinking, strongly conscious of the irreducible contingency of human events. Hence his emphasis, instead, on power, which is conceived as a group's sheer ability to overcome and neutralize any resistance by other groups to the realization of its own interests (material or ideal), or indeed to make the energies and resources of other groups serve those interests.

So understood, power is a thing – better: a relationship, for it results from the discrepancy between one group's capacity to assert its own interests, and that of one or more other groups – which has no other ground and justification than itself, and reveals itself merely as a matter of fact, not as the expression of that group's superior human merits.

This is particularly evident when we are dealing with politico-military power, which is grounded in organized violence, and asserts itself (when necessary) in the fact that a given group can confront and defeat another in the field, or can suppress the attempt by another group to subvert (again violently) the established order. In both situations what matters is the quantity of resources each party can commit to violent action, *plus* the respective capacity to mobilize and engage those resources, with the added component of causality, of luck or ill luck, or of destiny, which has often played a particularly evident role in military confrontations. In Weber's view, in the determination of outcomes, there is no significance attached to the effort made by contending parties – before or after the settling of accounts – to assert the intrinsic validity and justness of their own interests, and the superiority of their own ideals.

However, not all power is politico-military. According to Weber, two other forms of power exist, each grounded in a group's control over resources different from those on which organized violence rests, and on its ability to put them to use in pursuing its own interests. The first form, economic power, is grounded in resources related to the production and distribution of material wealth. A group which strategically appropriates such resources in a given situation can strongly limit the autonomy of other groups by excluding them from access to these resources. This can induce them to enter the market as bearers of less significant resources – typically, labour power – and thus to accept subordination in their economic activities.

The second alternative power form can be conceptualized only through a lengthier and more complex argument. Let us recall the central motif of what we have called Weber's philosophical anthropology. Constitutionally, human beings are thrown into an intrinsically disordered reality but cannot survive in it. They react to this situation by selecting certain aspects of it and imputing to them a meaning which is intrinsically arbitrary, and which can assist them in orienting their own action only if that arbitrariness is not acknowledged. This contradiction can be overcome if those meanings are seen as expressing a necessarily good and truthful, superhuman will, and as reflecting a transcendent rather than empirically accessible order, whose justness and validity individuals cannot deny.

As will be seen in chapters 4 and 5, Weber's sociology of religion analyses the ways in which such concepts have been elaborated and conveyed by the great 'world religions'. It emphasizes the differences between their messages and the different ways in which each seizes the central aspects of reality, and orients the conduct of individuals to the message of each religion. Here, however, we are interested not so much in the content of those messages, as in the way a message establishes itself as valid in a given situation.

This outcome has a key role in determining the relations between *Stände*, the groups operating as 'carriers' of one or the other of such message. Each group may operate within the context of both cooperation and competition with others; but each *Stand* aims to assert itself as the bearer and the medium of a message which deserves to establish itself as superior to all others. If it attains this aim, it becomes the source of a particular, possibly unique, authoritative definition of what is and what ought to be, a definition as far as possible accepted and shared across society.

In pursuing that aim, competing groups can avail themselves of varied resources, including politico-military and economic ones. However, another distinctive resource is a group's capacity to project as *sacred* its own understandings of reality – its own values – and to posit them as premises and standards of everybody's activities. Thus, in the competition, the symbolic aspect is critical. To become the winner, and particularly to *remain* the winner, a group must assert that its own world views and its own patterns of individual conduct – its own 'style of life', as Weber says – are uniquely valid representations of the transcendent order, conforming with its features and its commandments.

Optimally, in fact, all styles of life, not only those of the winning group, ought to function as symbolic vehicles of that order, representing the value hierarchies and the understandings of reality it expresses. Understood in this manner, in a given society all lifestyles, considered as a unitary whole, become a status system – an ordered complex of differentiated and hierarchically arranged social positions, each characterized by specific claims and obligations, privileges and burdens. Individuals derive a stable and generally acknowledged identity from the position they hold within this complex. Those who occupy the same position are thereby soldered into an exclusive, strongly characterized stratum. All such strata, together, form an ensemble which is publicly recognized and generally validated.

To the extent that this happens, we may say that a specific form of power (much less visible than the politico-military or the economic form) lies in the hands of a group which holds a distinctively prestigious position within the status order. It is identified as the prime source and medium of a message that is widely recognized as uniquely valid – as a particularly compelling way of interpreting reality and of establishing what conduct is expected of individuals.

Class, estate and party

To summarize: according to Weber, power takes three main, distinctive forms. All rest on a group's ability to appropriate significant social and cultural resources, and to employ them in order (so to speak) to put into a corner the groups deprived of them. They differ, however, according to the nature of the resources in question – respectively, means of coercion in the case of politico-military power, means of production in the case of economic power, means of interpretation in the case of a third power form, which we may call ideological. Again, note that this formulation on the one hand echoes the Marxist emphasis on the significance of resources and their appropriation, but on the other hand objects that resources other than economic ones also matter, and should not be considered derivative and secondary in relation to those.

The chief Weberian text that suggests this formulation, *The Distribution of Power in Society: Classes, Status Groups and Parties*, is a brief, unfortunately unfinished, essay (or chapter), the opening sentence of which states forthrightly that 'classes, estates, and parties are phenomena of the distribution of power within a community' (Whimster (ed.) 2003). Classes form in the sphere of economic relations, and especially of market relations. Whether an individual enters the market as the owner or *not* owner of capital differentiates the most significant classes, but further differentiations are possible. For instance, individuals who do not possess capital, but possess knowledge, skills or other qualifications critical for the production of goods, or the rendering of services, find themselves at an advantage in relation to those who possess only unskilled labour power. The individuals' class position directly affects what Weber calls their *Lebenschancen*, the opportunities open for their existence.

Estates (but the standard English translation of *Stand* in this particular meaning is 'status groups') form in the sphere of social and cultural relationships. Individuals belonging to different estates typically enjoy different amounts of prestige, or of moral credit. Each estate is characterized by a different *Lebensstyl*, 'lifestyle'. The lifestyles of different estates stand in a hierarchical, and to an extent invidious, relation to one another. But taken together they express shared cultural values, agreed understandings of reality and conceptions of a dignified human existence.

The power component in the relations between estates is particularly in evidence when a superior estate can exclude the others from access to goods, practices or forms of knowledge which it itself enjoys. It can command others to keep a respectful distance and to perform certain services for, thus recognizing the superiority of high estates and the inferiority of low ones. But often there are multiple, subtle gradations in the ways that each estate, even a relatively under-privileged one, defends whatever privileges it possesses from even less privileged ones. (It has been said that the system of ranks typical of the European *ancien régime* was like 'a cascade of contempt'). Historically, estate orders ('status systems') have established and maintained themselves in remarkably different ways. The system characteristic of medieval Europe, in particular, was juridically sanctioned, and took the form of distinctive sets of rights and duties vested in the individual. In the Hindu caste system, what separated the castes from one another was a system of ritual sanctions, centring on the question of pollution.

Finally, parties form within the sphere of political relations, which, as we have seen, result from the differential access of groups to means of coercion. Often, however, ongoing political relations do not expressly refer to or deploy organized violence, which is brought to bear relatively seldom, as a kind of last resort. Normally, parties differ chiefly in the extent to which they can (or cannot) exercise influence on the formation and implementation of policy. Thus, a party – in a broad sense of the term – is a group characterized by the capacity it may or may not have of asserting its own interests by determining or influencing the content of binding public commands.

Note that these three 'power groupings' – classes, estates, parties – can coexist in a given historical context, and affect different aspects of it. They represent, respectively, the ways in which wealth is created and allocated within it, the distribution of the publicly recognized claims of individuals to a quantum of prestige, and the ways in which public faculties and facilities for command and sanction are assigned or denied to individuals. As a result, a given individual may find himself sharing his class position with certain other individuals, his estate position with others, and his party positions with yet others. In other words, within a given society, classes, estates and parties may cut across each other; and a given individual may find himself favoured concerning one kind of power, and disfavoured concerning the others. On this account, it is often said that Weber advances a multi-dimensional view of social inequality, in contrast with the one-dimensional view held by Marx.

Weber and Marx

Let us reconsider briefly the relationship between these two great social theorists, synthesizing Marx's thought by means of one of the first sentences in the *Manifesto of the Communist Party*: 'all history hitherto is the history of the class struggle'. I suggest that, if Marx himself read that sentence to Weber, he would object: 'Indeed, Dr Marx. But not *the whole story!*' Let us clarify this objection.

First of all, even if we focus on the conflictual aspect of historical developments, it is not right to consider classes as its sole protagonists. Classes, as we have seen, emerge within the sphere of economic relations. Marx and Weber see them somewhat differently, for the former emphasizes the relations of production, while the latter emphasizes those taking place on the market. Weber would concede to Marx, however, that classes have played a fundamental role in the historical process, and particularly do so in modern society. Here, according to Weber, secularization decreases the significance not only of religion but also of other social and cultural phenomena of a symbolic nature, and in particular of *status* as the instrument and the stake of relations between groups.

However, for Weber, history also displays the strategic significance and resultant conflicts of groupings different from classes, and thus of estates and parties, which operate, respectively, in the spheres of socio-cultural and political relations. Furthermore, that sentence from the *Manifesto* places excessive emphasis on the phenomenon of conflict, regardless of its protagonists. The conflicts themselves have mostly yielded, through their resolution, to durable phases of reciprocal accommodation. Such accommodations have mostly proved unstable in the long term, but they have often structured the relations between groups in the short and the middle term. They have engendered commonalities in defining reality, organizing existence, prescribing and sanctioning practices through ethics and law, and in pursuing aesthetic, intellectual and religious values.

As we shall see, Weber attaches particular importance to commonalities of a political nature. Although polities are structured primarily by the division between those who govern and those who are governed, and although the privilege of governing is the object of conflict between parties, a given polity can, under certain conditions and to certain effects, constitute a generally recognized, legitimate order, which has at its base a political community – typically, in the modern world, a nation. The polity serves as an instrument of the nation in its pursuit of distinctive collective interests, chief among these being its greater might and security vis-à-vis other polities. Although pursuit of these interests may generate contention among polities, such contention may sometimes lead to relatively durable alignments between some of them.

This in no way makes irrelevant the question, which *Stände* have primarily affected the formation of the arrangements and rules of a given society, and which *Stände* these favour. Weber pondered this question, not only as a scholar but also as a citizen of his native Germany during the Wilhelmine era. As we have seen, his answer criticized the national bourgeoisie, of which he was a member, for its unwillingness to challenge either the political predominance of the Junker element or the excessive role played by dynastic interests and by court circles in determining the foreign policy of the empire.

More generally, Weber held that for certain purposes it was apt to claim that different European populations possessed different 'national characters'. However, he refused to attribute them, as many were doing at the time, to each population's ethnic composition, or even to its biological make-up, considered distinctive for each 'race'. Rather, in his view, national characters were the contingent, not-necessary product of the historical resolution of serious conflicts, sometimes remote in time, between the *Stände* active within a given society. Typically, such resolution involved the victory of one *Stand* over others – for instance, the victory of the Roundheads over the Cavaliers in the English Civil War. This determined the prevalence of a culture, and of a particular complex of understandings and values, which in the long run became *the* English culture, and in this capacity formed the character of the English nation as a whole.

We have discussed in this chapter so far how, for Weber, individuals are the ultimate referents of both sociological and historical discourse, acting within a context that is formed by, among other things, groups of individuals. As we have seen, the same can be said of groups. They, too, operate in the presence of other groups and interact with them. But group interactions are in turn partly occasioned, structured and mediated by relatively constant and self-standing features of the context as such – in particular, by its institutions. Given certain conditions, the outcomes of group interactions congeal, so to speak, in codes, arrangements, resources, expectations, rewards and sanctions. From a certain point, these in turn orient and control further group interactions, and through these affect, and sometimes modify, the characteristics of the groups in question.

Relationships between institutional spheres

Many of the typologies that were developed in *Economy and Society* – which in my judgement represent some of Weber's most significant legacies – present distinctive ways, each relatively coherent and stable, of solving a given problem. In dealing with that problem, each historical context privileges one of these ways, in a more or less close approximation to its ideal-typical version. Since the problems themselves are many, the context derives its physiognomy from all the solutions preferred for them.

Economy and Society generally does not indicate which *Stände* are primarily responsible for the solution imparted in a given context to a given problem, and how they imposed their preference on other *Stände*. More than in the historical events involved in those processes, Weber is interested in the characteristic features of a given solution, the conditions requiring or facilitating its adoption, and its consequences, together with the adaptations which it underwent subsequently. Above all, he seeks to show how the solutions found for different problems limit one another, and what indirect effects, respectively, the solutions *a*, *b* or *c* of problem A produce for the solutions *u*, *v* and *z* of problem B – and vice versa.

In this manner, it is possible to address questions such as the following. Within religious cultures, which conceptions of the road to salvation are compatible with, and perhaps conducive to, which solutions to 'the problem of evil' – and vice versa? Which kinds of judicial procedure and which ways of training lawyers and judges must be adopted within a country's legal system in a country seeking to promote industrialization? Is it equally possible to confer political citizenship on individuals where the most significant socio-economic inequalities lie between social classes, *or* where they lie between castes?

As one can see, in this kind of analysis it is not necessary to ask oneself systematically what the subjective orientations characteristic of given individuals or groups may be, nor to ask which cognitive and moral perspectives are reflected in given institutional arrangements or in given complexes of ideas and values. Weber's interest, instead, chiefly concerns the relations between arrangements and between complexes. He asks what boundaries the solution given to one structural or cultural problem lays on another problem.

Furthermore, without expressly declaring this or justifying it theoretically, Weber takes for granted that all the social systems he deals with – essentially, *whole societies*, that is, relatively large, relatively durable and relatively autonomous systems – must deal with a limited number of great themes on which social relations and cultural phenomena are focused. The themes are those of religion, politics, the economy, sexual and parental relations, science and technology, and law.

To this extent, one may say that Weber conducts a functional analysis, oriented to the problems of a social system considered as a self-standing unit, except that he does not see that society as a harmonic whole which dictates to its subordinate parts its own preferred solutions to its problems.

On the contrary, although most of the contexts envisaged by Weber are whole societies, he uses the expression 'society' relatively infrequently, and perhaps unwillingly. The term *Gesellschaft*, which he derives from Tönnies, and which can be translated as 'society' or 'association', is juxtaposed and counterposed with the term *Vergesellschaftung*. This refers not so much to a self-standing social entity as to the process in the course of which a set of social relations takes on a more and more 'societal' or associational shape. (This is the case, in particular, when traditionally oriented relations are supplanted by rationally oriented ones.)

In Weber the social whole does not find its configuration by imposing on its parts determinate (and necessarily similar and compatible) ways of confronting such general themes as religion or politics or by making the *Stände* active in the respective spheres serve its own needs. On the contrary, that configuration is largely the contingent, unplanned product of the encounters, clashes and accommodations between the strategies the *Stände* themselves undertake on behalf of their 'material and ideal' interests, which are the product of priorities engendered across a society by those encounters, clashes and accommodations.

This emphasis on the role of the *Stände* should not be taken to suggest that Weber ever forgets the subjective makings of the relations into which they enter. At bottom, the factors involved are always, in an American sociological dictum, *things that people carry around in their heads*. In one of his most impressive analyses of the relationships between institutional spheres – the so-called *Zwischenbetrachtung*, a lengthy essay translated into English as *Religious Rejections of the World and Their Directions* – Weber insists on the conflictual nature of those relations. But here his argument starts from the necessity for individuals to orient their own existence, in order to impart meaning to it, to *one* overriding value. It refers chiefly to the incompatibilities between the values central respectively to the religious and moral sphere on the one hand, and the spheres of politics, the economy, the aesthetic experience, the erotic experience, and science on the other hand.

Basically, Weber argues that one cannot serve two masters. Whoever seeks to attend to the same extent and to devote the same energy, in her own existence, to more than one of those competing values, runs the risk of devaluing all of them, thus depriving her own existence of a centre and of significance. (As it happens, this is exactly what *l'homme moyen sensuel* seeks to do – he negotiates and makes compromises between various aspects of his existence in order to moderate or mask the tensions between the relative values.)

Thus the compatibilities and incompatibilities, the reciprocal constraints which lie between the institutional arrangements of a given society, have an existential resonance for the individuals on whose actions and passions all those arrangements rest. Even in dealing with 'the state', Weber reminds the reader that such a massive, complex and imposing ensemble of arrangements exists only if and to the extent that in their reciprocal actions innumerable individuals abide by certain expectations, in order to validate *certain* ways of forming, implementing and obeying political decisions – the ways characteristic of state-ness.

To bring the discourse back to the level of the individual, seeking to understand (*verstehen*) his subjective processes is also necessary, or at any rate useful, in order to accord with an aspect of Weberian social theory that lies, apparently, on a different level. Weber does not subscribe to any theory of history which attributes to it a single, univocal direction and meaning, and considers it as a single riddle capable of (and indeed destined for) a single solution. He cannot subscribe to such a theory because of his strong sense of the intrinsic contingency of historical events. According to him, even historical trends of great duration whose continuation is apparently most assured could turn out to be reversible, given appropriate (and in turn unpredictable) conditions. This view accords, again, with Weber's philosophical anthropology. If all meaning is subjectively conferred on events, and thus open to contestation, this applies also to the meanings which scholars claim to detect in human events, and particularly to the values they seem to affirm.

Rationalization

For all this, Weber does identify and conceptualize certain tendencies of historical development which manifest themselves in innumerable events, over long stretches of time, and which affect multiple aspects of social existence. In particular, he acknowledges that the advent of modernity has deeply impacted on many social structures and forms of culture, and in the course of a few centuries, has displayed a persistent dynamic. Starting from its original base, Western Europe, modernity has affected successive spheres of existence in one part of the globe after the other.

Furthermore, Weber conceptualizes this development as a particularly coherent and powerful expression of a specific modality of human activity – the rationalization of forms of thought and activity. And this is just *one* expression, for there have been other, different paths to rationalization, focused on this or that sphere of existence, and inspired by this or that way of conceiving, conveying and realizing rationality.

To clarify this Weberian position, it is appropriate – and perhaps necessary – to return to the level of individual action. Consider Weber's most general typology, mentioned in the previous chapter. On the basis of the subjective processes orienting it, all action can be subsumed under one or the other of four ideal types: traditional; affective; value-rational; and instrumentally rational. One can then conceptualize the rationalization process in these terms. Over time, the two types of rational action displace and replace the traditional and the affective type, or at any rate reduce its significance for the social process in general.

This can happen in various ways. For instance, in a given society the practice of agriculture may cease to be guided chiefly by the appeal to the traditional wisdom conveyed to peasants, say, by proverbial lore, and come to be increasingly oriented to the findings yielded by systematic experimentation, undertaken perhaps by a specialized public agency. Alternatively, agriculture may continue to be chiefly oriented by tradition, but lose significance, either within the economy as a whole or in comparison with commerce or industry – two forms of activity intrinsically more open to expressly rational conduct.

Let us consider further this elementary account of the Weberian view of rationalization as the master process of modernity. More and more frequently, in their various activities individuals comply with a model of deliberate action, undertaken and managed in the light of self-consciously apprehended objective circumstances. They seek to attain the objectively optimal ratio between the means at the actor's disposal and his ends – regardless of whether these, in turn, are also self-consciously chosen, or have been imposed on the actor by an overriding commitment to a superior, unchallengeable end.

The relations themselves *between* actors reflect this model. Increasingly, such relations are formed with a view of specific ends, which the actors implicitly or explicitly communicate to one another, negotiate and agree upon. Actors are expected to consider those relations themselves as means to the agreed ends, and to manage them in the light of express codes of conduct, which do not allow much leeway to tradition or spontaneous affect. They, instead, pursue those ends by employing the most effective technical instruments available in the context because, operating within it, are other groupings formed by actors in sustained relations with one another, and all such groupings often compete or conflict with one another. This implies, among other things, that alignments and contrasts based on status become less significant than those grounded in the possession of (or exclusion from) economic resources, together with the relative interests, or those based on access to positions of political power. To employ the tripartition presented before, estates become recessive, while classes and parties become dominant.

These social aspects of rationalization, as well as the political ones that are related to the increasingly central position of institutions of a *state* nature (as we shall see in chapter 7), are accompanied by congruent cultural aspects, in complex and controversial causal relationships with the social ones. In particular, secularization reduces the credibility and the effectiveness of religious values and views which for centuries, in the Christian West, had placed the sacred at the centre of the universe, of both individual existence and public life, and had generally affirmed and celebrated the authority of tradition.

That authority is also increasingly challenged, in the cognitive realm, by the growing authority of science. This constitutes an ensemble of empirically grounded *savoirs*, ever open to increase and to revision, and capable of orienting more and more effective techniques for exercising control over nature (and society). Within the moral realm, individualism asserts itself. It enjoins the single individual, in seeking to orient her activity, to appeal mainly to her own judgement and her own interest, and asserts the moral validity of this principle.

Weber attributes to these rationalization processes, considered as a whole, an epochal significance. Although historically unique, and although originating in a single part of the world, Western Europe, over the last few centuries they have acquired what we would today call global significance. Their effects extend to the most remote regions of the world, inducing people to turn their backs on their own local traditions, and to conform with a single model.

Getting this process under way has been the peculiar historical mission of the West, argues Weber in his introduction to the edition of *The Protestant Ethic* published in 1920. Starting with classical Greece, through various developments in Rome and in the Middle Ages, but with particular urgency and vigour from the beginnings of modernity, the West has been the region of the world where new, expressly rational ways of performing a number of social and cultural tasks, in the most varied fields, have been discovered and tested. Although developed in a particular region, while also deeply rooted in the Western historical experience, these ways have gained universal dominance and have corrupted or replaced alternative ways of pursuing those same tasks. Paradoxically, then, the historical peculiarity of the West lies in its *not* being peculiar, for its distinctive material, institutional and cultural products have, in the course of the century, followed a global, unifying and uniforming trajectory.

For Weber, however, the epochal dimensions of this whole story, and the fact that the rationalization processes originating from the West have not exhausted their effects, but indeed continue to advance, do not constitute 'the end of history'. This expression, not to be found in Weber but paraded by some authors since the publication of Francis Fukuyama's essay of that title in 1989, has two main meanings. First, history constitutes the unfolding of a dynamic intrinsic to it, which may realize itself through multiple, varied and sometimes surprising developments, but works towards a predetermined fulfilment. Second, at a certain point this fulfilment is attained, and from that point history no longer holds any surprises.

Weber denies (implicitly) both meanings, for they contrast with his profound conviction of the intrinsic contingency of human events. In the first place, these obey no compelling logic. Even the West has fulfilled its peculiar vocation only as a result of a complex constellation of multiple causal effects, taking advantage of diverse and casually converging circumstances. Furthermore, even a trend as powerful and lasting as modern rationalization can be interrupted, diverted or inverted by a sudden turn of events. There is always the possibility – and there are many historical precedents – that from a relatively remote corner of the earth a new message may emerge, which denies any moral validity to rationalization and condemns its advances instead of celebrating them. And such a message can find an audience in which it evokes a committed following, with collective energies capable of challenging and subverting a line of development which had long proceeded unchecked. (This possibility lies at the centre of the Weberian conception of charisma.)

There are reasons for considering such a turn to be possible – if not probable. For one, in its lengthy advance the rationalization process marginalizes and sacrifices incompatible values, but cannot entirely suppress their appeal or the nostalgia that is evoked by their memory. In the first two decades of the twentieth century, Weber gave considerable attention to social and cultural movements which sought to contrast the dominant values and tendencies of bourgeois culture, asserting that it was vacuous, exhausted, corrupt and inhuman.

Generally, Weber considered these movements (youth movements, movements inspired by Nietzsche or Freud, or aesthetic movements) unlikely to attain their goals, or disapproved of those goals. Yet they confirmed for him a thesis related to his philosophical anthropology, and which his historical-comparative study of religion was also confirming. Values, world views or attributions of significance to life (and death), being intrinsically arbitrary, are by the same token multiple and diverse, or even incommensurable and incompatible.

On this account, according to Weber, the intellectual and moral perspectives underlying the development of Western modernity could not claim to be uniquely valid, and necessarily rooted in reality. In any case, history, as well as the growing knowledge of non-Western societies and cultures, revealed that there currently existed, or had existed in the past, institutional arrangements and cognitive and value systems different from the modern, Western ones. This entailed the existence (at any rate virtual) of a *variety pool*, a set of alternatives on which further history could continue to draw.

Even assuming provisionally that the advance of rationality would continue to characterize ongoing events, we have seen that rationality is possible in two variants – one oriented to values, and one instrumentally oriented. Modernity seemed to have largely opted for the latter, but by the same token it left open an option for the former. Furthermore, Weber remarked, Western rationality was largely intended to control, manipulate and master nature, which was seen as a set of mere givens – a distant and foreign 'Other'. (In this respect it is interesting to recall Descartes's view of man as *maître et possesseur de la nature*.) Classical Chinese culture, as we shall see in chapter 5, proposes an alternative model of rationality – one that prefers to reflect and adapt to reality, by acknowledging, imitating and protecting the harmonies intrinsic to nature, instead of superimposing upon it an imperious will to power.

Finally, Weber had an acute sense for the complexity of social events, and for the possibility that an apparently unitary phenomenon contains discrepancies and tensions between its various aspects. Earlier in this chapter I explored the connection with the rationalization process of both the moral code of individualism, and the growing tendency to establish and manage social relations on the basis of rational criteria, primarily by seeking an optimum ratio between the costs and the benefits of effort. Now, this second tendency finds its most clear expression in the formation of bureaucratic systems, which progressively come to control collective activities within an increasing variety of contexts, from political parties, to firms, to hospitals, to armies, to churches. Such systems, however, leave less and less space for the cultivation and expression of modern value orientations such as the individual's autonomy, risk-taking and responsibility.

This paradox raises a problem: which of the contrasting tendencies will prevail? Weber seems to have foreseen (with dismay) that in the long run the bureaucratic tendency would prevail upon and jeopardize individualistic values. But he was far from considering this as a foregone conclusion. Rather, he used the concept of charisma to point out the possibility of the sudden and irresistible breakthrough of a cultural and social movement that could challenge the inertia of structures (both traditional and rational, and in particular bureaucratic structures) that were apparently as solid and as durable as rocks.

Even aside from such considerations, on two other accounts Weber would not have subscribed to the idea of 'the end of history'. First, modernity encompasses aspects which by their very nature produce intrinsically contingent and unpredictable results. Think, in particular, of two closely related realities: science and technology. Modern science rests on (or indeed consists of) an institutional mechanism for the production of ever new findings, many of which in turn lend themselves to surprising technological innovations. But, alongside this, the great political machine of the state, and the associated great administrative machine of bureaucracy, tend to push their own boundaries, taking on ever new tasks and absorbing ever more resources.

In the second place, we may mention one further characteristic of many of Weber's 'ideal types'. These not only indicate the structural features of a given arrangement, but also reveal the recurrent problems it must confront, and the tensions that exist between some of those features. For example, all charismatic domination is beset by two contrasting necessities: to confirm its own legitimacy by maintaining its dynamic, attaining ever new successes, *and* to achieve some measure of stability by (among other things) limiting the inevitable risk of failing to succeed.

Thus, different aspects of its institutional physiognomy push charismatic domination in different directions, and at best this continuous tension can generate an unstable equilibrium. The same can be said of most systems of political domination, where on the one hand the centre seeks to establish its control over its own agencies in the periphery, and on the other hand these seek to reduce that control and to assert their own autonomy.

'Unstable equilibrium' does not mean continuous shifts from one prevailing tendency to the other. Rather, each prevalence is continually threatened by the possibility of the other, and must keep it at bay through strategies which may, at some point, fail to produce the desired effects, or produce (together with those, or without them) unwanted ones. Also, for this reason, Weber's methodological preference for 'ideal types' of arrangements which intentionally stylize them and reduce their number, does not invalidate historical reality or deny its fluidity. It affirms instead its intrinsic (though not always apparent) disposition to change, in directions wanted or unwanted, and thus its irreducible unpredictability.

In summary, Weber's conception of socio-historical process anchors it in a multiplicity of individual actions, each oriented (also) by what goes on within individual minds. However, he does not, on this account, view that process as a Brownian motion of a relentless vortex, where myriads of unrelated initiatives, attempts, successes and failures collide randomly, signifying nothing. The mental operations themselves which inspire and orient the individuals' activities do not spring out of a vacuum. They are de-randomized by the fact that they relate to data, conditions and values, which constitute the historical precipitate of the action of groups held together by, and operating on behalf of, collective interests. For, as we have seen, the actors that matter historically are *Stände*, groups, each encountering others and confronting them in order to assert in their presence, and, if necessary at their expense, its own material and ideal interests, by shaping context which it can share with the others, but in a position of advantage. And the results of the whole process, concerning both structural arrangements and cultural contents, are systematically upheld.

It is impossible for all groups to enjoy this privilege. *Which* do, in a given situation, depends on the quantum of power each one possesses – and whether it is grounded in a group's ability to apply superior force, in its control over strategic material resources or in the acknowledged moral superiority of a group's way of living and conducting itself.

Societies are the most significant contexts within which the outcomes of the interaction of groups are crystallized, regardless of whether these interactions are conflictual, competitive or cooperative. Each society is characterized by the ways in which recurrent social and cultural problems are resolved within it, namely, those concerning religious, political, economic, juridical and aesthetic matters.

The concrete means of resolving these problems vary, because they are historical products, connected with the here-and-now of specific circumstances. But the variety of approaches can be reduced conceptually to relatively small sets of 'ideal types', which serve to 'triangulate' both the initiatives and strategies of various groups and the configurations which their relations impart to the society as a whole. Considered over long periods, such configurations can reveal continuous and coherent changes in a given direction. According to Weber, in the case of the West that direction can be conceptualized as a sustained rationalization of social relations and of cultural contents. But that tendency must again be considered as the product, partly non-intentional, of the actions and interactions of groups – not as the manifestation of an immutable and irreversible destiny that is immanent in the historical process.

4
The Protestant Ethic and the Spirit of Capitalism

Weber and economics

Only in 1908 did Weber publicly define himself as a sociologist, and his subsequent references to this characterization of his scholarly activity were rare, and did not conceal his reservations concerning it. That activity remained, in fact, highly diverse both in its methods and in its themes, and was never limited by close observance of the conventional boundaries between disciplines.

In addition, Weber had a rather unconventional approach to the discipline of economics, with which he was officially identified throughout his career – at Freiburg, and subsequently at Heidelberg, Vienna and Munich. Even in a late and very significant text (the opening of *Science as a Profession*), he used the expression 'we economists'. And yet, it was remarked by Schumpeter, authoritatively and without ill will, that this eminent scholar made no significant contribution to the science he professed – at any rate if one adopts the contemporary meaning of 'economics'.

One might paraphrase Clemenceau to suggest the reason for this: according to Weber, the study of economic phenomena was too important for it to be left to economists. At any rate, the technical aspects of the scientific study of economic phenomena held little interest for him, particularly given the way the so-called marginalist revolution was redefining the scope and method of the discipline, first in England, and subsequently in Austria.

On the other hand, three sets of *lato sensu* economic themes, which that revolution tended to bypass, were of great interest to Weber. In the first place, the *history* of economic phenomena, and particularly that of capitalism and industrialism, were distinctly modern developments, which, by affirming the autonomy of economic processes from other social processes, had rendered the first particularly dynamic. The second set to interest him concerned the nature of *economic institutions*, that is, those highly variable sets of rules, arrangements, resources and practices within which economic activities are conducted. Third, the *relationships* between economic institutions and other social institutions, especially religious, political and juridical ones, were of particular interest to him.

Weber made highly original contributions to these three sets of themes, and in the process he became a most significant practitioner of economic sociology. There are overlaps between those sets, but by and large one can assign to one or another of them the contributions mentioned below.

Weber contributed to the field of economic history by writing scholarly monographs on the economy of classical antiquity (see his books on the agrarian history of Rome and of other parts of the ancient world) as well as on that of the Middle Ages (the dissertation on early forms of commercial partnership). Furthermore, he taught an extensive and demanding course on economic history at Munich, shortly before his death; we know the content of those lectures because some students took shorthand notes which were edited into a book after his death (Knight (ed.) 1927, 1950). In particular, this work provides a detailed discussion of the rise of the modern economy and the course of industrialization.

Between 1908 and his death Weber worked hard to plan and edit a large set of volumes on the social aspects of economic activity, exploring both strictly economic processes and the varied social or cultural processes which either assist or limit the former. Although the history of this project is complex and problematical, within the context of it he reserved for himself a theme which encompasses those of many other volumes, as is indicated by the title of the resulting,

unfinished book – *Economy and Society*. Here, economic institutions such as money, taxation and wage labour are systematically discussed. In each case, the analysis has a historical
dimension, but the prevalent mode of treatment is the elaboration of conceptual typologies. However, these also address
aspects of social existence which are not, themselves, economic
in nature – for instance, politics, religion and law.

Finally, the massive set of Weber's essays on the sociology
of religion starts with a question: in the history of the greater
civilizations, what have been the prevalent relations between
the economy and religion? To rephrase this in terms already
employed in this book: how have expressly *ideal* interests,
such as those dominant in the religious sphere, interacted with
markedly *material* interests, such as those dominant in the
economic sphere? More narrowly – to what extent, in various
parts of the world, have ideas and practices of a religious
nature assisted or hindered that transformation of economic
structures and processes which characterizes modernity?

Weber's perspective on the religious phenomenon

Here, we shall deal only with this last theme, and do so select-
ively. The writings that concern us reflect Weber's assumption
that the sociologist ought to pay attention to the contents and
the forms specific to each religion. Religions *matter*, both historically and within the individual's experience, not only
because of what they all have in common, but also because of
what makes them different from one another. What is of interest is, chiefly, the diversity of ways in which religions shape a
view of the world and locate human beings within it, expressing a determinate conception of the limitations and the potentialities of an individual's existence.

This approach to religion is less obvious than one might
expect, at any rate within the context of scholarly reflection
on social and cultural phenomena. Chiefly, it differs from two
alternative approaches. In the first, what matters are not so
much *religions* as *religion* itself, the former being considered
as individually insignificant variants of the latter. Those variants all perform the same function; they create a degree of

homogeneity within the moral orientations and the views of reality held by those who belong to one and the same society. In the second approach, one should not attach much significance either to different religions or to religion itself, for all manifestations of the religious experience basically reflect and mask those social inequalities which chiefly structure the relationships between a society's constituent groups.

However, in keeping with his philosophical anthropology, Weber attributes a significant role to the complexities of meanings harboured in the minds of individuals, for they establish some order within the intrinsically disordered reality into which all human beings are thrown. But that role is performed in a variety of ways from one complex of meanings to another, and those variations, in turn, largely reflect the contents of culturally and socially different religions.

Thus, Weber's sociology of religion is to a large extent a sociology of religions. To use an expression of William James's, but with an alternative meaning to the one he intended, these are focused on 'the varieties of religious experience'. On this account, Weber often pays much attention to the intellectual substance of different religions – their creeds and their theologies. He attends to the ways in which each religion describes and prescribes the individual's position and role in the cosmos, relates her to the Deity, orients her conduct in this world and inspires her perception of her destiny in the afterlife.

Largely for this reason, Weber's great essays on the sociology of religion deal with what he called the 'world religions'. These are religions *of the book*, which have produced and transmitted rich and varied intellectual patrimonies, and have entrusted their continuity to elaborate institutional arrangements (beginning with a variety of expressly religious roles). In the course of their history, they have entertained (and theorized) complex and diverse relations with other major aspects of society and culture. On the other hand, relatively few texts of Weber's (contained mostly within *Economy and Society*) deal expressly with the religions of what used to be called primitive peoples, those chiefly studied by anthropologists.

A word of caution, however: if Weber pays much attention to the specific contents of different religions, this does not mean that he attributes to them a direct and predictable impact on structures and processes pertaining to other spheres of existence, and particularly to the economic sphere. In fact, the world religions have not, themselves, paid much attention to economic affairs. Actually, it is only with the start of modernity that economic affairs have established their distinctiveness and autonomy with respect to other cultural and social concerns – particularly sexual relations, kinship or politics – that have always been perceived as significant by world religions. In any case, to the extent that religious beliefs and practices have had an impact on economic activities, that impact cannot be traced simply by considering how such activities have been expressly described, prescribed, justified or condemned by those religious beliefs and practices. Largely, it has been mediated by the sometimes complex and paradoxical effect of such beliefs on other, diverse aspects of individual and social experience, and particularly by the way this effect has oriented what Weber call the *Lebensführung*, the conduct of existence.

Modern capitalism

To appreciate this and other aspects of Weber's discourse on religions, let us consider briefly his most famous work, the essay *The Protestant Ethic and the Spirit of Capitalism*, published in 1904–5 and republished in 1920, after Weber (a few weeks before dying) had revised the text in order to include it within the first volume of his collected essays on the sociology of religion. The essay not only bears on the sociological topic of the relationship between religion and the economy, but also on economic history, for it addresses one aspect of a development of the greatest historical significance – the genesis of modern capitalism – and discusses its causes.

First, let us consider what it is all about. Weber, together with other authors, but not with Marx, held that there had been significant forms of capitalism before modernity, but that the latter had been characterized in a radically new form. What *is* modern capitalism according to Weber? The answer given below was derived by Johannes Winckelmann (responsible for all editions of *Wirtschaft und Gesellschaft* after the first, edited by Marianne Weber) from numerous passages in the Weberian writings.

It is a capitalism oriented to production, which operates by means of firms, and functions on the market. It has the following features: 1. Fixed capital, invested in the production of goods on which depends the satisfaction of the daily needs of the masses. 2. Material and organizational means of production are wholly appropriated by the owners of capital. 3. There is rational capital accounting, oriented to long-term profitability, to the capacity to produce and reproduce profits. 4. Orientation to the opportunities present on the market. 5. Rational organization of labour and of the work discipline. 6. Rational technology. (Weber, *Wirtschaft und Gesellschaft* (Tübingen: Mohr, 1976, 3 vols): 101; the passage, by Winckelmann, is an annotation relating to p. 369 of vol. I)

This system dominates the whole landscape of the modern economy on a world scale – in Weber's time nearly as much as in our own. Profit-oriented production by means of wage labour marginalizes or subordinates to itself all other ways of organizing productive activities, in particular, those aimed at rendering the producers self-sufficient, that is, able to survive chiefly from their own products. Producers, instead, must now depend for the satisfaction of their needs on the disposal of those products and the acquisition of those of others.

Historically, capitalism owes its success to its unequalled capacity to rationalize the processes of production and distribution, for it is only by acting on such a basis that economic units can remain on the market, and remunerate both their owners and their workers. But capitalism has achieved its dominance starting from a situation where it did not exist at all, or had at best a marginal and subordinate existence with respect to other, traditional ways of organizing and managing those processes. Thus, there is definitely nothing *natural* to its presence in the modern environment. This poses a historical problem of the first magnitude: to what circumstances, to what complexes of events, does capitalism owe its genesis?

In *The Protestant Ethic* Weber seeks to give a particular, original and grounded contribution to the solution of that problem. Thus, he takes for granted many other contributions to it that are established components of the genesis of modern capitalism. Among these, he takes for granted many elements of the solution advanced by Marx, stressing the role played by changes in the means of production, by their appropriation on the part of capitalists, and by the relations between the appropriators and those they employ in the production process. Alongside such considerations, *The Protestant Ethic* accepts, and indeed emphasizes, other, not expressly economic components of the genesis of modern capitalism – for instance, the availability, in the historical context of that genesis, of particular institutional and intellectual resources, such as relatively rational arrangements for the adjudication of disputes and the conduct of political activities, or mathematical notions and practices amenable to the management of economic activities.

Early capitalist entrepreneurship and its spirit

The Protestant Ethic fits its own argument within this complex vision of the genesis of capitalism, and adds to it by focusing on a specific component of that genesis – early capitalist entrepreneurship. This is the *collective* subject, responsible for the historical task of identifying and mobilizing the new economic resources, and realizing the opportunities for gain which the institutional and intellectual arrangements of early modernity offered. I stress 'collective' because Weber dissents from other economic historians, who attributed a most significant role, instead, to just a few *larger-than-life* individuals, who had displayed great imagination and daring in specific commercial ventures, amassing great fortunes, and thus (it was held by some) had single-handedly placed modern capitalism on the map.

For Weber, however, this historical task could only have been achieved by a relatively large number of individuals, characterized and to an extent unified by shared perspectives and modes of activity. It was a matter, first, of constructing a bridgehead within the pre-modern economic system for a new way of generating and managing wealth, followed by a progressive consolidation and widening of that bridgehead until it could subvert that system, replacing it with one possessing the entrepreneurial characteristics of modern capitalism.

Thus *The Protestant Ethic* does not discuss the whole process of modernization of the European economy. Within this very large theme it selects a relatively narrow one, the nature of the social group which constituted the protagonist of that process. Furthermore, it does so from one specific viewpoint. In dealing with the early capitalist entrepreneurship Weber does not address its social composition, its geographical distribution or a number of other potentially relevant aspects. Again, in keeping with his philosophical anthropology, he asks himself instead which complex of shared meanings, of understandings of reality, may have oriented the activities of that group, validating these activities morally and intellectually, to inspire and justify it in the performance of its historical role. He senses that those who collectively experimented with and developed those new and disruptive ways of producing and distributing wealth, by creating and managing enterprises, had been motivated by a *spirit* different from that which had previously been shared by economic agents – a distinctive *capitalist* spirit.

This historically novel set of meanings, appropriate to the new economic games of modernity, had not only placed the seal of its moral approval upon the acquisitive aspirations of individuals, but had also induced them, or indeed compelled them, to pursue those aspirations through their untiring, methodical, day-to-day activity. On the one hand those individuals were enjoined to manage as rationally as possible the resources they invested in the enterprise (beginning with their own energy, their self-discipline and other strictly personal capacities), while on the other hand they were enjoined to seek ever new products, new markets, together with new social and material technologies of production and distribution.

In this context, other authors had emphasized the practice of keeping separate accounts for the patrimony of the entrepreneur and his family on the one hand, and for the enterprise on the other. Weber suggests that this practice was not just a useful, or perhaps indispensable technique of management, but also had moral significance. It required the individual entrepreneur to engage himself steadily and consistently in a demanding and stressful task. He was to pursue the growth of the capital of the enterprise continuously and systematically, and abstain from expending in consumption the returns of any of its market operations, committing them instead to ever new operations. In a word, his attitude towards his own wealth was to be one of *stewardship*.

More generally, according to Weber, the spirit of capitalism was a set of injunctions which appealed to the individual's sense of *duty*. It was a code which did not accommodate itself to his will but laid boundaries on it, forming an imperious standard against which to test his moral mettle. The task of inserting the foreign body of capitalism into the economic structures of early modernity, which would later be un-done and then re-done in its image, with capitalism in a position of dominance, could only have been performed by a set of individuals who not only took advantage of new opportunities for gain, but *in the very process of doing so* verified and improved their own moral standing, and whose existence reflected in all its aspects a new sense of how an upright, responsible person *ought* to act.

Let us review some aspects of this new 'spirit':

- a prevalent appeal to rationality as a criterion by which to orient to reality and make choices;
- a corresponding rejection of the assumption that the traditional way of doing things is intrinsically valid and deserves to be respected;
- a repression of the tendency to act in unreflected response to emotional impulses, including such noble ones as love for fellow humans, compassion for people in deprived and needy conditions or solidarity with one's associates; in principle, that conduct is valid vis-à-vis persons *a* which is valid also vis-à-vis persons *b* . . .;
- one's conduct should encompass a medium to long-term orientation, which requires controlling one's impatience and fatigue, or any tendency to take shortcuts towards goals or to slacken one's striving towards distant objectives once proximate ones are achieved; on the contrary, each attained objective should be viewed as a means to the attainment of further ones;
- a disposition to assess the moral validity of one's conduct in the light of its demonstrated capacity to yield objectively verifiable results;
- a preference for objectives, the attainment of which lends itself to calculation, where that calculation in turn takes into account the relationship between resources expended and objectives attained;
- an openness to experimentation and innovation.

According to Weber, these are aspects of an action orientation which is loaded with moral significance, such that their sustained presence in a given individual's activity confers meaning to that individual's existence. It remains true, however, that the presence of those traits, when an individual is an entrepreneur, reveals itself chiefly in monetary gain, although this is supposed to increase that individual's capital rather than being used for consumption.

Religious implications of the capitalist spirit

The reference to monetary gain as the measure of one's moral status raises a problem, and finally leads us to what is often referred to as *die Gretchenfrage*, echoing Margaret's question to Faust regarding his stance on religion. And, as summarized below, Weber argues, that Christian principles relating to work and gain were still dominant in late-medieval, early-modern Europe:

- the systematic seeking after material gain was regarded as morally damaging, or at any rate dubious;
- the pursuit of worldly goals in general, and particularly of those related to the economic sphere, was considered less valid, from a religious viewpoint, than pursuits directly related to the search for salvation, such as spiritual contemplation, prayer and the practice of virtue;
- individuals compelled by their own circumstances to invest much energy in worldly practices such as labour, were enjoined to adapt to and respect traditional patterns of activity, framing it as the fulfilment of the duties attached to one's ascribed rank;
- more generally, a strongly positive view of tradition was held, as a source of guidance for action both in general and in the economic sphere and thus the practice of innovation and experimentation was discouraged.

How, then, in a context so characterized, could the spirit of capitalism assert itself, prevailing upon such strong reservations of a religious nature?

The Protestant Ethic presents an answer to this question. The formation of the capitalist spirit had required favourable conditions in the economic sphere; and the Protestant

Reformation had put those conditions in place. In some parts of Europe (precisely those where modern capitalism had first manifested itself), the reformed Christian confessions had denied religious sanction to the principles listed above. But they had not done so (at least in the first instance) by liberating economic activity from any previous religious constraint, or by locating it within a purely secular and earthly view of reality. They had not authorized individuals to throw themselves into economic activity without any fear concerning their fate in the afterlife, or any felt need for justification. On the contrary, in the context of early modernity that fear and that need continued to be urgent and compelling. In fact, both the fear and the need were closely connected with the new moral statute of economic activity.

So far, Weber's thinking does not differ from that of many contemporary authors who had asserted that Protestantism had played a key role in the advent of modernity. (They took pride in such assertions, because they shared a negative attitude towards the Catholic tradition which the reformed confessions had attacked and transcended.) The title itself of Weber's essay may suggest a relationship between the capitalist spirit and the Protestant Reformation taken as a whole, in all its forms. But the title masks a critical difference between Weber and those other authors. Weber attached much weight to the diversity within the organizational structures and creeds of various religions. Thus, in the case of reformed Christianity, he questions *which* among the several confessions has performed *which* historical role, and for *which* reasons. His treatment of this question is at the heart of *The Protestant Ethic*. It is complex (and controversial), and to simplify it I will emphasize the contrast he posits between two answers.

First, Weber rejects the answer most common among German scholars, according to which the Lutheran Reformation had played the decisive role. Curiously, that answer was foreshadowed in a passage of Marx's *Capital*, to the effect that Luther had indeed dissolved the monasteries, but at the price of transforming all believers into monks. For Luther had enjoined all individuals, in attending to their worldly tasks, to maintain that assiduous dedication which had once been required only of monks.

Without referring to Marx's suggestion, Weber dissents from it. True, Luther had attached much moral significance to the concept of *Beruf* (vocation), which he had introduced in the first German translation of the Bible. But he had conceived of *Beruf* in an essentially static manner, and had underwritten the traditional medieval exhortation to the individual: fulfil conscientiously the duties of your status; abide by and be content with your social rank; identify yourself with your trade and comply with the rules of your guild. Clearly such exhortation, if applied to the conduct of a business, could not have lent a religious sanction to the spirit of capitalism.

The role of Calvinism

The Protestant Ethic presents a different, original solution: that historical role had been performed by Calvinism. This was a particularly radical reformed confession, which had originated from French Switzerland, and had subsequently found many followers, particularly in Holland and in England (where it had been called Puritanism, the name it bore also in the American colonies). Again, Weber pays much attention to the theological content of Calvin's version of Christianity, and particularly to one, highly distinctive component of it – the dogma of predestination.

According to Calvin, God has decreed for each human being, from all eternity and for all eternity, its destiny in the afterlife – salvation or damnation. If he is a believer, each individual knows that he has been the object of such a decree, but cannot know its content, much less make a difference to it, for Calvinism radically 'disenchants' the world. That is, it denies the believer any chance to ascertain or interfere with God's own inscrutable designs by means of sacramental practices, since Calvinism has no place for such practices, and considers them as forms of magic. Even believers, therefore, are denied any opportunity to have access to God's will concerning them, to atone for their sins or to gain God's benevolence. They can hope to be among those souls which God has destined to salvation – the elect – but cannot count on that.

According to Weber, this generates in the Calvinist faithfuls a painful solitude, with a besetting anxiety for which there is no remedy according to their faith itself. However – he argues – the pressure of those feelings is so strong and persistent that it induces them to seek a way, no matter how implausible from the standpoint of orthodox belief, of reassuring themselves as to their destiny in the afterlife.

Typically, the way is the following. The faithful commits all his energies to managing his own life, day by day, in a strenuously assiduous, watchful and rationally controlled manner. He does so, principally, in carrying out the mundane tasks of his occupation, his *Beruf*. This becomes, then, the central aspect of his whole existence; it transforms the typical Calvinist believer into a *Berufsmensch*, a person fully identified with his occupation, and who (without any express theological warrant for this) views his success in it as an indication of his own good standing in the eyes of God, guaranteeing his destination of salvation in the afterlife.

One might say that Weber corrects Marx's dictum, reported above, and suggests that it was not Luther but Calvin who made a monk of every human being. More precisely, he states that Calvinism engenders a new form of asceticism. The traditional Christian asceticism was *other-worldly*; it was practised in the monasteries by small numbers of individuals who, in the hope of gaining salvation through their conduct, fled the challenges and temptations of the mundane existence of common people. The new ascetism is instead *this-worldly*, for it is to be practised by individuals who do not seek an escape from the banal circumstances of normal existence, but commit themselves to mastering their callings.

This new asceticism constitutes 'the Protestant ethic' – one which takes very seriously the daily, mundane tasks of individuals, enjoining them to pursue such tasks with great energy and dedication. But such dedication is of a different nature from the mere fulfilment of the traditional duties of one's station recommended by Luther, for, paradoxically, it entails a measure of detachment. Mastering one's calling requires, in this new understanding, a willingness to challenge and modify, leaving behind the conventional ways of practising it in order to improve on them. It also requires a kind of detachment from other individuals with whom one associates in the practice of one's calling, whether as customers, collaborators or competitors. Above all, the mastery of one's calling requires a continuous, tireless commitment, which becomes almost an end in itself, and to that extent acquires a positive moral significance.

As one can easily see, this ethically loaded way of conceiving and conducting one's *Beruf*, if practised in the context of occupations of a commercial and productive nature, *becomes* 'the spirit of capitalism'. It informs the particularly demanding, assiduous and rationally oriented way of building and managing businesses, which, according to Weber, was typical of the early generations of capitalist entrepreneurs. It morally authorized them, so to speak, to unmake and remake the economic structures and processes of early European modernity. The moral mortgage laid upon economic activity by traditional Christianity (in its Lutheran version, too, Weber insists) was thus replaced by a Christian conception that placed a high value on the sustained, rational practice of that activity.

Energetic and clever individuals – provided of course that they possess other resources quantitatively and qualitatively appropriate to business pursuits – can avail themselves of the new opportunities for profit offered by the material and institutional arrangements of early modernity. They can do so, claims Weber (1930: 176), not only without risking moral jeopardy, but indeed 'with an amazingly good conscience'. Indeed, in the success of their business undertakings, they can see both a test of their moral stature and an indication of their status as elect in the eyes of God, or at any rate express and by the same token release their concern with that status.

Weber's thesis

This is, then, the 'Weber thesis'. It establishes a strong relationship, indeed a causal one, between two ideal constructs: upstream, as it were, Calvin's conception of spiritual salvation; downstream, the spirit of capitalism. *The Protestant Ethic* does not expressly argue, but assumes, that Calvinist populations constituted a privileged terrain for the emergence of early capitalist entrepreneurship. Many studies have subsequently thrown doubt on that assumption, locating the rise of modern capitalism in other regions of Europe, or in phases of European history which either preceded or followed the phase emphasized by Weber (the seventeenth century). Or they have suggested that other religious groups, or indeed social groupings without a religious identity, constituted the *milieux* within which early capitalist entrepreneurship developed.

In fact, this controversy, which began even before *The Protestant Ethic*, was stimulated by its appearance, then engaged Weber's energy for several years in a confrontation with his critics, and is still continuing, three generations later, with or without an express reference to the 'Weber thesis'. I shall not even try to settle it on its merits. Instead, I have sought to convey only the theoretical import of that thesis, which I would recapitulate as follows.

The genesis of modern capitalism required, among other conditions of a very different nature, the formation of a spirit compatible with or indeed conducive to this new way of managing economic activities. Such a spirit would not only allow entrepreneurs to systematically orient their conduct to gain, but would enjoin them to do so on the one hand in the most rational ways, those most open to innovation, and on the other with a sense of assurance concerning the moral validity of those ways.

The formation of such a spirit, and its adoption by relatively large groups of early entrepreneurs, in turn required the elimination of strong religious impediments. A particular religious vision, Calvinism, especially via a peculiar and salient component of its beliefs – the dogma of predestination – performed this historical operation, albeit through a complex and counter-intuitive causal itinerary. Thus a phenomenon which belongs straightforwardly in the religious sphere played a significant, though partial, role in the emergence of a phenomenon central to the economic sphere, which subsequently affected many other aspects of modern social existence, first in Europe and then in the rest of the world.

We can consider some of those effects as a form of feedback, in that they took place in that very sphere of religion from which the process had started. They are largely paradoxical (or indeed perverse) effects, for they had a negative impact on the vitality of that sphere. First of all, even within the first few entrepreneurial generations – for whom (according to Weber) the individuals' dedication to the spirit of capitalism had been more or less directly motivated by their belief in predestination – the very success of their professional activities progressively deadened the religious nerve of some individuals; it rendered less cogent and constant their concern with the question of salvation, and weakened their identity as believers.

In the second place, and more importantly, in the course of becoming the central economic fact of modern life ('the most fateful force' of it, according to Weber), capitalism contributed powerfully to the advance of secularization and the Church became less significant as a collective protagonist of the general social process. The world view and the moral values of Christianity (in all its variants) lost salience and credibility in modern Western culture, or at any rate ceased to be the most relevant component of it.

The complex constellation of causes and effects in the development of modernity presents, in Weber's argument, a further paradoxical aspect. After contributing significantly to the *genesis* of capitalism, the capitalist spirit (which is not only a set of recommendations that the entrepreneur follows because they work, but is also a set of commandments, compliance with which assures him of his moral standing and thus empowers him) ceases to be necessary for the *functioning* of the capitalist system.

Weber (1930: 181) makes this point in a lapidary manner: 'The Puritan *wanted* to be a man identified with his calling – we *have* to be.' The system continues to require certain practices, and the performance of these is utterly necessary for the individual if he is simply to survive as an entrepreneur – if he does not perform accordingly, he will inexorably 'go to the wall', a victim of the competitive process.

5

Other Essays in the Sociology of Religion

Weber and Marx again

One significant theoretical import of *The Protestant Ethic* is a partial but pointed critique of Marx's thought. There, interests and resources of a non-material nature – in particular, those of a religious nature – could only be assigned a secondary and derivative role within the socio-historical process, particularly when this showed momentous changes. However, *The Protestant Ethic* argues against such a view. Although it does not oppose the materialistic view of history with an idealistic one, it locates its thesis within a broader interpretation of the genesis of modern capitalism which amply acknowledges the significance of properly material factors.

Furthermore, in his historical-comparative essays in the sociology of religions, written between 1910 and 1920, Weber takes up a theme which echoes a Marxian view, according to which individuals' location within a given society, and in particular its system of economic inequality, conditions (if it does not strictly determine) their cultural orientations, including those of a religious nature. In those essays Weber suggests that different *Stände*, whose collective identity is fixed in the first instance by their position in a society's division of labour, also derive certain forms of religious sensitivity and experience from this position, including certain ways of understanding and relating to the Deity in myth and ritual.

This point is best made in the opening pages of the introduction to *The Religious Ethic of the World Religions*, an essay also published in English as *The Social Psychology of the World Religions*. Here Weber indicates which strata have played the most significant role in the development of each of those religions. In particular, Confucianism can be considered as the ethic of a distinctive status group (about which more is said later in this chapter), the mandarins, men whose extensive (and expensive) literary education – once verified by demanding examinations – qualified them for the tenure of administrative positions in the Chinese empire.

The mandarins' predominantly secular, rational orientation to the management of worldly affairs markedly differentiated them from the protagonists of the development of early Hinduism – the Brahmans, members of the highest caste. These were also men of literary education, familiar with ancient Sanskrit texts, but who did not usually hold administrative offices. Rather, their function was to provide spiritual and ritual advice to individuals and communities, especially concerning the obligations and entitlements of the members of various castes. In later times, the development of Hinduism also drew on different kinds of religious personnel, who practised particularly strenuous forms of ascetic conduct or addressed the religious needs of the lower strata.

Buddhism found its 'carriers' chiefly in monks oriented to mysticism and contemplation, who had no homes and begged for alms while wandering. Islam, on the other hand, was originally the religion of a body of conquering warriors, resembling a Christian knightly order such as those that existed during the Crusades, but lacking their sexual asceticism. Later, they were flanked by the practitioners of Sufism, a variant of Islam oriented instead to mysticism, but again without undertones of sexual denial, and practised by brotherhoods of traders and artisans.

Weber characterized Judaism, as practised in the diaspora after the Jews' exile from Palestine, as the religion of a town-based people having a 'pariah' status, for its believers were excluded from normal social intercourse with the dominant Christian population. Under these conditions, the dominant religious role came to be held by a distinctive Jewish group – intellectuals trained in biblical and Talmudic literature and

ritual, yet with a rationalistic orientation, who were sometimes located in a semi-proletarian role and sometimes in a
petty-bourgeois role within the social hierarchy.

Christianity began to perform its historical role as the religion of travelling craftsmen and journeymen, says Weber, and
it developed as a distinctly city-based and city-oriented religion, although it had very different social embodiments –
from the primitive communities of believers, to the mendicant
monastic orders of the Middle Ages, then to the confessions
and sects of reformed Christianity.

As if to refute those who saw *The Protestant Ethic* as an
idealistic alternative to Marx's materialistic view of history, in
this and other ways Weber investigates what he calls 'the other
side of the causal chain' (an image I have never found particularly appropriate) – that is, the impact of material factors
upon religious ones, rather than the opposite theme, developed in *The Protestant Ethic* itself. But the text in question
goes on to state expressly that each religious ethic, no matter
how influenced by social (and particularly by economic and
political) factors, expresses an authentically spiritual intuition
and religious inspiration. In other words, religious innovation
is always the outcome of one or more individuals' original
confrontation with arduous ethical and existential problems,
and, in the first place, its further elaboration is a response to
the religious needs and demands of later generations. None of
this excludes the fact that social and cultural interests of a
non-religious nature may exercise a strong influence – sometimes a decisive one – on the structure of religious groups and
even on the content of their doctrines.

The historical vocation of the West

The essays on 'the economic ethic of the world religions' complement the earlier essay in a further sense. In *The Protestant
Ethic* Weber had attributed a significant role to Calvinism in
the development of the capitalist spirit, and thus in the genesis
of modern capitalism. The later essays argue that, in other
parts of the world and in other phases of history, some religions
had prevented the emergence of something like this-worldly
asceticism, and thus of the spirit of capitalism. By the same

token, those religions had denied moral legitimacy to groups that expressed an interest in promoting something similar to modern capitalism, thus rendering them unable to perform that role. To paraphrase a slogan of the 1960s: a religion that was not part of the solution was part of the problem.

But *which* problem? Those essays not only discuss the genesis (or failed genesis) of modern capitalism, but also consider this topic as one aspect of a broader theme – the specificity of the whole historical experience of the West. At one point Weber had become aware that modern capitalism itself constituted the expression of a broader phenomenon in the sphere of the economy (Marianne Weber, in the biography of her husband, speaks of this as his 'discovery'). This rationalization was the vocation of the West – its tendency to favour, in all aspects of its social and cultural identity, modes of thinking and acting of a rational character, rather than modes inspired by respect for tradition or those allowing the spontaneous expression of emotions. In the pursuit of that vocation the West had served as the proving ground of multiple, diverse innovations (technical, political, scientific, aesthetic, juridical and institutional). These, thanks to their greater capacity to render efficient and predictable the workings of the respective spheres of social existence, had subsequently extended their reach to other parts of the world. Here, they progressively weakened and displaced the previously dominant ways of constructing and managing those spheres.

Weber develops this argument expressly and succinctly in his introduction to the first volume of the collected essays on the sociology of religion (1920). This is an important text (some commentators claim that it states *the* central theme in Weber's social theory) but if read alone it can lead to some misunderstandings. To appreciate correctly the notion of rationalization as the vocation of the West one must bear in mind several points.

Weber chiefly contrasts the rationalization process, in whatever sphere, with traditionalism. He does not consider the recourse to reason as the criterion for action and thought as valid in itself; but it functions as a social and cultural strategy whereby tradition can be put on the defensive, overcoming (to a greater or lesser extent) its inevitable opposition to social and cultural change.

Rationality and rationalization are two highly abstract expressions, and each can be understood in various ways. According to some Weberian texts, what is peculiar to the West is *a certain type* of rationality, characterized by the effort to control and mastery reality (Descartes spoke of man as the master and possessor of nature) and to render action as effective as possible, as well as predictable in its results. One may contrast this with another type of rationality, which has a less commandeering and manipulative relation to reality. This type seeks, rather, to attune itself to reality, and to echo the harmonies which are intrinsic to it (consider the difference between a Chinese and a 'classical' French or Italian garden). One could also say that this second type of rationality is less likely than the first to inspire a *rationalization project*.

A further, related, difference is the following. We have seen that according to Weber there are two forms of rational action. One is both committed to and constrained by a certain value or set of values, which it respects absolutely and to whose exclusive pursuit it dedicates itself. The other is not so committed and constrained, but is totally instrumental. This duality is reflected also within Western rationality. For instance, according to an example of Weber's, the main Western traditions of juridical thought and practice are all rational. But one may contrast the rationality of modern, positivistic legal thought, which aims to maximize the predictability of the juridical consequences of transactions and judgments, with the rationality of Canon law, applied by ecclesiastical courts. Here, rationality is bounded by the unchallengeable priority of one value criterion: the *salvation of souls*. If strict juristic discourse leads to a conclusion which threatens that value, that conclusion must be overridden.

Finally, Weber does not consider the appeal to rationality, and the prevalence in the Western experience of material and institutional structures oriented to it, as proof of the intrinsic superiority of that experience. He is too aware of the limitations and contradictions of rationality (consider the paradoxes mentioned in the last chapter), and of its human costs. On this last account, in an unfortunately unfinished statement, Weber gives a conceptual portrait of the market, acknowledging its merits as uniquely conducive to economic efficiency, but exposing its potentially frightening moral implications.

Furthermore, he holds that the preference for rationality (and even more so for any one conception of rationality) as the supreme criterion for action and thought cannot be rationally justified. Essentially, it is itself an irrational or at least an a-rational option, a value choice.

The economic ethic of world religions

Weber's comparative-historical researches on the sociology of religion developed these and other insights through an extensive discussion of the 'world religions'. As Weber says in an opening statement:

> By 'world religions', we understand the five religions or religiously determined systems of life-regulation which have known how to gather multitudes of confessors around them. The term is used here in a completely value-neutral sense. The Confucian, Hinduist, Buddhist, Christian and Islamist religious ethics all belong to the category of world religion. A sixth religion, Judaism, will also be dealt with. It is included because it contains historical preconditions decisive for understanding Christianity and Islamism, and because of its historic and autonomous significance for the development of the modern economic ethic of the Occident – a significance, partly real and partly alleged, which has been discussed several times recently. (Gerth and Mills (eds) 1946: 267)

Although Weber did not live long enough to bring this formidable research project to its conclusion by writing at length on Islam and on Christianity (initiated in *The Protestant Ethic*), his collected essays on sociology form a monumental work, mainly because they deal systematically with other topics than their fundamental theme, the 'economic ethic' of those religions. This is constituted by 'the practical impulses to action' which religions produce not so much through their explicit teachings on economic matters, as through their 'psychological and pragmatic implications'. It is through these that religion impinges on 'the conduct of existence' (*Lebensführung*) of individuals, particularly as concerns their occupational activity, and especially their business practices.

However, the essays also encompass aspects of culture and of social structure – respectively, of Imperial China, pre-colonial

India and ancient Israel – which are rather remote from that theme. Suffice it to say that the essay on the religions of China (including both Confucianism and Taoism) opens with a discussion of the monetary system of the celestial empire! As a result, intentionally or not, each essay yields a relatively comprehensive view respectively of the Chinese, Indian and Jewish civilizations, laying special emphasis, next to the religious components of each, on the dominant forms of social inequality related to those components.

However, I do not intend to provide a succinct review of the results yielded by this immense research endeavour, which analyses many of the most significant socio-cultural experiences of humankind from a comparative-historical perspective. Below, I limit myself to a summary account of one essay, dealing with the Chinese empire, and do so exclusively with reference to the problems set out originally in the context of *The Protestant Ethic.*

The Chinese experience

There is a good reason for focusing on China. According to Weber, Imperial Chinese society presented aspects which *might* have allowed it to experience and promote rationalization processes comparable with those which *did* take place in the early modern West, culminating in modern capitalism (and the modern state).

Let us consider first some structural aspects. The Chinese empire had a very long (and tormented) history. It survived serious conflicts over political power, repeated 'times of troubles' marked by the dispersion of that power, difficult successions between dynasties and barbarian invasions. During the long stretches between these episodes, however, it constituted a vast but relatively centralized and stable system of domination, centred on the figure of the emperor himself, but articulated into relatively well-marked territorial sub-units. These were administered by a large but homogeneous body of skilled administrators – the mandarins.

The imperial territory had long contained cities, markets and guilds of merchants and artisans. Chinese agriculture, thanks to the exemplary industriousness and ingeniousness of the peasants, had high levels of productivity, allowing it to sustain a large and growing population. The access to the mandarin stratum and its privileges depended in principle not on ascriptive criteria, but rather on the evidence aspirants gave, through their performance in a series of highly competitive examinations, of having assimilated a very large literary heritage – a task requiring, to begin with, the mastering of a great number of characters in a difficult script. Finally, at times when the West still availed itself of relatively unsophisticated technologies, Chinese civilization presented highly advanced and complex technologies, in fields as diverse as the construction and management of large irrigation systems, metallurgy, textiles, chemistry and ceramics, as well as the production of books and other objects that rendered a comfortable and attractive existence for the upper strata.

If we consider, next, some cultural aspects of Chinese civilization, we find some that might have *authorized* the development of something like the spirit of capitalism, with its appreciation of worldly values and its encouragement of the systematic rationalization of economic processes.

The central inspiration of Chinese culture had been given in the sixth century before Christ by the great thinker Confucius. Confucianism (which Weber decided to characterize as a religion) was a vast body of sapiential learning, containing directives for correct ritual and correct practice, with insights into the nature of reality and into the proper relations among human beings. Those who aspired to mandarin status had to assimilate Confucian doctrines, through a lengthy and arduous educational process. Those doctrines were supposed to guide and inspire the practices of the mandarin stratum, orienting in a coherent manner its handling of essential political and administrative tasks. Entrance into the mandarinate depended on success in exams which tested the applicants' knowledge of a large body of classical texts, beginning with Confucius's own writings.

Thus, at a time when the selection of leading personnel in Europe largely depended on birth, and often rewarded the skills of illiterate warriors, the Chinese empire was run essentially by literati, cultured individuals, men of learning, selected chiefly for their intellectual achievements and tested by competitive examinations. Furthermore, the knowledge imparted by the Confucian *cursus studiorum* was predominantly of a secular nature; the classical writings did not have a metaphysical, highly speculative, theological content. Many dealt with questions of ritual, but the dignified, stylized behaviour they prescribed chiefly expressed a worldly ideal of self-control, correctness, aesthetic appropriateness and thoughtful deliberation. The Confucian wisdom did not refer expressly to the wishes of a deity, did not prescribe magical practices and did not articulate other-wordly justifications for the conduct it enjoined or recommended. Finally, Confucianism expressly avowed mundane values such as physical health, longevity, material well-being, a moderate search for physical and artistic pleasures, accord between one's aspirations and activities and the harmonies of nature, as well as orderliness and equilibrium in one's existence and in the management of public and social concerns. In this sense, the message of Confucius and his associates and followers was rational in nature – although it bespoke a rationality that respected and reflected reality, and adapted to it, rather than mastering it.

If these structural and cultural aspects of Imperial Chinese society might have served as a context for processes similar to those characteristic of Western modernity, others, however, could be expected to hinder such processes. Chinese towns, for instance, were numerous, rich and well-populated, and harboured an advanced division of labour. But they never enjoyed juridical, military or political autonomy from the rest of the empire's territory; nor did they impart to towndwellers a privileged citizenship that transcended their bonds towards their village of provenance and their kinship group. There were intense traffics over the imperial territory, but there was not a unitary body of commercial law, or a coherent system of coinage and of credit consistently framed and backed by the imperial centre.

The dominant social group was constituted by the mandarinate, which linked that centre with the huge periphery of the empire, thanks to its monopoly over administrative services and the related opportunities for gain. Thus, the fortunes accumulated by merchants were often expended in funding the very expensive preparation of their children for exams that would lead (if successful) to entry into that group, and/or in the purchase of land; they were not committed to further accumulation and investment in traffics and commercial acquisition.

Puritanism and Confucianism

Within the complex of factors which, on balance, kept Imperial China from becoming the site of a dynamic process of economic modernization, Weber emphasizes those which pertain to the subjectivity of actors, to their conceptions of a morally valid and dignified existence. He stresses some fundamental differences between Puritanism (in the book on China he prefers this expression to Calvinism) and Confucianism, which explain why Confucian rationalism, unlike Puritan rationalism, did not engender or endorse a rationalization project.

Which differences? In the first place, Puritanism stressed the radical distance and difference between God and the world, and thus induced in the believers themselves a sense of detachment and tension, or indeed opposition, towards the world as it exists. This is seen as a realm shot through with finitude and sin, and thus open to human action, to a contingent 'doing and undoing' on the part of individuals, which glorifies God to the extent that it is dynamic and successful. Whereas, Weber argues, Confucianism has no place for a notion of the world and those who inhabit it as intrinsically sinful.

An American commentator of Weber's, of Chinese origin, echoes this strong contrast by narrating a presumably autobiographical episode:

> A young and proud Chinese college boy was travelling on a steamer along the China coast in 1933. He was leaning on the railing of the deck and gazing at the sunset when an American Baptist missionary picked him up for a likely object of conversation by walking up to him and suddenly declaring, "Young man, you are full of sin, you need to repent." The young man was surprised with shock, and yelled back declaring: "I come of reputable ancestry, I have a good conscience, and I have always been strict about my moral responsibilities and conduct. How is it that I am full of sin? Maybe you are full of sin, but I am not." (Yang, in Weber (ed. Gerth) 1951: xxxix)

This difference points to another, perhaps more fundamental one, which separates Confucianism and Hinduism from Judaism, Islam and Christianity. In the Oriental conceptions of the cosmos, of the universal ordering of things, there is no place for a personal God who addresses his divine commandments to human beings, expecting them to be obeyed. As Weber writes, in the Confucian vision in particular:

> [t]he impersonal power of Heaven did not "speak" to man. It revealed itself in the regimen on earth, in the firm order of nature and tradition, which were part of the cosmic order, and . . . in what occurred to man. The welfare of the subjects documented heavily contentment and the correct functioning of the order. (ibid.: 28)

Furthermore, Puritanism radically disenchanted the world, denying any validity to magic (even as represented by Christian sacraments), for it saw magic as an attempt to manipulate and modify the relationship between the individual and the Deity. On the contrary, Confucianism, despite being a sapiential doctrine that did not authorize magical practices, had always allowed them to be pursued in the Chinese empire, in the context of Taoist and Buddhist religions, as well as within numerous forms of folk religion. Furthermore, it approved of the cult of the ancestors. Thus, the Puritan universe differs significantly from the Confucian universe, in that it is strictly monotheistic.

A further, related difference is shown by a theatrical text of early Scottish Puritanism, bearing the title *Everyman*, which suggests that this new version of Christianity is addressed to everybody, without distinguishing between the mere faithful and other, 'charismatically qualified' personnel, such as monks, nuns or priests. Confucianism, instead, has always been the specific cultural patrimony of the Chinese literati, that is, of a privileged stratum distinct from the masses – although its doctrines affect those masses by orienting the mandarins' administrative practices. In this manner, they impart to the existence of the population at large a relatively diffuse and coherent moral tone.

Let us re-state two reasons why Confucian rationalism does not sustain a project of rationalization. First, it encompasses

a conservative orientation towards existent reality, an accep-
tance of the established order of things, a diffidence towards
innovation. In the second place, Confucianism acknowledges
and validates a marked distinction between those who have
learned its doctrines and practise them in their daily life, and
the rest of the population, who are allowed to continue practising magic and other folk cults which are not open to rationalization. As a result, tradition, or indeed multiple traditions,
remain the chief source of orientation for the daily activities of
the masses, beginning with those concerning labour, production and acquisition. (Even in contemporary China, Western
observers often remark with surprise on the role played, in the
activities of successful entrepreneurs and managers, by practices of geomancy and of divination, intended to keep at bay
or to conciliate potentially hostile spirits.)

Of course, in other historical situations, too, tradition
maintains its hold on the daily life of the masses, including its
economic aspects; and this certainly happened in late-
medieval and early-modern Europe. Here, however, at different times and to a different extent in various parts of the
continent, economic modernization, and signally the advent
of modern capitalism, first contrasted, then expressly challenged and subverted, the dominance of tradition in the life of
the masses themselves. According to Weber, this fundamental
historical operation had found its 'carrier' (*Träger*) in early
entrepreneurship, whose activities were oriented by the capitalist spirit, an expression (in turn) of this-wordly asceticism.
There was no place for such a group within the multisecular
history of the Chinese empire.

During those centuries an estate of literati maintained its
privileged position, both because of the prestige of its intellectual patrimony, and because it monopolized the administrative
positions responsible for overall management of the empire
itself. And the literati were a *non*-productive estate, which
lived off prebends or benefices, exactions that were levied more
or less officially from the flow of tributes that went from the
empire's periphery to the centre, in the form of 'gifts' extracted
from villages. Their lifestyle reflected a great consideration for
wealth, well-being and material comfort; but it was not compatible with a sustained, assiduous and absorbing commercial
or productive activity that was oriented to competition, to

technical innovation, and to the opportunities for profit and investment present on the market.

The Chinese literatus viewed himself and handled himself, as far as possible, as a cultured human being, a 'gentleman' who in his daily life pursued an ideal of poise and equilibrium. Such a gentleman would show a conscious dedication to intellectual and aesthetic values, to virtues (such as filial piety, respect for the aged, subjection to superiors) and to ritual codes that echoed and affirmed tradition, the established political and social order, and the harmony of the cosmos. Also, in matters of policy and administration, this conception opposed any attempt to systematize and rationalize such values through projects of reform and innovation. In any case, such projects were out of the question in the economic sphere.

The last few pages of *The Religion of China: Confucianism and Taoism* emphasize the contrast between this conception and the one represented by the Puritans. The latter considered himself as the instrument of God who, distancing himself for the world, leaves its destiny entirely to man. The individual could thus work in and on the world to the full extent of his personal capacity, and see in the success of his operations the measure of his own moral stature and an indication, however indirect, of his status as one of the elect. He thus becomes a *Berufsmensch*, a man identified with his profession or vocation. The Confucian 'cultivated man', however, does not consider himself as an instrument: 'he adapts himself to the world and seeks his own perfection as an end to itself, not as a means to a functional goal' (ibid.: 256).

In summary, although the Confucian world view is rational in character, which in turn inspires a rational ethic, this is less coherent and radical than the rational Puritan ethic. Only the latter promotes the relentless rationalization of existent reality that is suited to the entrepreneur's tireless and methodical effort in the pursuit of accumulation and profit that constitutes the subjective dimension of modern capitalism in its early phase. According to Weber, the lack of anything similar within the millenary story of the Chinese empire contributed to the exclusion of a comparable experience for the Chinese, in spite of factors that might have favoured it.

In this sense, Weber considers his exploration of Chinese religions, together with two other Oriental ones (Buddhism and Hinduism), as an additional proof of the central thesis in *The Protestant Ethic*. To reiterate this: only a relatively large social group, possessing not only certain material resources, but *also* a conception of economic activity which morally justifies the search for profit, and which is in turn religiously inspired, could be empowered to defeat the economic traditionalism of previous civilizations, making of labour and enterprise the fulcrum of a vast and dynamic rationalization process.

This thesis, in turn, echoes and confirms Weber's philosophical anthropology – the human being as an interpretive animal, positioning itself in the world (and indeed constituting a world) by attaching significance to selected aspects of reality. It also expresses the intuition presiding over his monumental study of the 'varieties of religious experience'. That is, historically, the task of shaping, expressing, codifying, transmitting and sanctioning the most important meanings by which humans have interpreted the cosmos, and their own position within it, has been performed chiefly by religion.

However, different religions have performed that task in many, and sometimes radically diverse, ways. In turn such diversity, together with other factors, has conferred on historical experience its distinctive richness and variety. Weber's commitment to this position is clear from the following quote from the introduction to *The Economic Ethic of the World Religions*:

> [T]he nature of the desired sacred values has been strongly influenced by the nature of the external interest-situation and the corresponding way of life of the ruling strata and thus by the social stratification itself. But the reverse also holds: wherever the direction of the whole way of life has been methodically rationalized, it has been profoundly determined by the ultimate values toward which this rationalization has been directed. These values and positions were thus religiously determined. Certainly they have not always, or exclusively, been decisive; however, they have been decisive in so far as an ethical rationalization held sway, at least so far as its influence reached. As a rule, these religious values have been also, and frequently absolutely, decisive. (Gerth and Mills (eds) 1946: 287)

6
Political Power and Legitimacy

Social power again

As we saw in chapter 3, Weber assigned a decisive role to social power in the relations between groups. Social power can manifest itself in different forms, since it rests on privileged access to resources which are themselves very different in nature – means of coercion, means of productions and means of interpretation.

This chapter and the next discuss the form of social power grounded on the means of coercion: political power. As we have already seen, political power constituted for Weber a theme of the greatest importance, initially from the standpoint of his personal values. His most intense concerns addressed the key theme of what could be called *high politics* – the competition among sovereign states over the respective might, for such might is the key means to securing the nation's most significant interests, if necessary by recourse to war. Too many times Weber saw these concerns of his being threatened by the mistakes of German political leadership in the Wilhelmine era, and, finally, he perceived the country's defeat in the Great War as a shattering personal tragedy.

But, also, within Weber's theoretical work and particularly in his conception of the socio-historical process, the political sphere held a central position, and his scientific writings deal more with this than with the spheres of religion or the economy. Towards the end of his life, Weber was planning a *Staatssoziologie* as a major work; and, according to one of his contemporary interpreters, Reinhard Bendix, political phenomena were intended to occupy a central position in the overall design of *Economy and Society* – a book that, as we know, he never finished.

Other interpreters throw doubts on this view, holding that even towards the end of his life Weber attributed a critical position to religious or to more broadly cultural phenomena. But no one doubts the importance of politics for Weber, not only as a citizen or as a publicist (see his collected *Political Writings*; Lassman and Speirs (eds) 1994), but also as a social theorist. It is equally obvious that his treatment of politics contains some of his most significant contributions to social theory.

In order to convey simply some of those contributions, let us return briefly to the theme of social power, particularly in the form of political power. Such form is grounded in organized violence, that is, on some people's capacity to awaken fear in others, putting at stake their survival and physical integrity. Weber says this expressly with reference to the state – the most important institutional expression of politics in the modern era – in the opening paragraphs of *Politics as a Vocation* (Gerth and Mills (eds) 1946).

This tough-minded view should be emphasized, because in some other writings of Weber, and in those of some of his commentators and interpreters, the notion of organized violence as the core aspect of political experience is sometimes rapidly sublimated into the theme of legitimacy. Although Weber did deal extensively and creatively with this theme, he reached it through a conceptual itinerary which some secondary literature neglects. I will recapitulate it, here, to suggest that legitimacy itself lies within a broader context, and that its significance should not be overstated.

A complex conceptual itinerary

According to Weber, a power relationship exists to the extent that, given two subjects who interact, but whose goals are in contrast with one another, one subject has a certain probability of realizing its goals even against the opposition of the other. However, in one of the passages in which he advances this definition, Weber observes that taken by itself it denotes a phenomenon which is rather too widespread and relatively amorphous. So understood, power can be held by a great variety of subjects, individual or collective. The occasions and the issues with respect to which it can develop and be brought to bear can be most varied. In a given interaction context, power so understood can shift, according to different circumstances, between one subject and another, and then vice versa. Sometimes, it affects interests of no great social significance.

Thus, from a sociological viewpoint, it is best to pay attention to situations characterized not so much by power itself as by domination (*Herrschaft*, which is often translated as 'authority') – situations, that is, where the power relationship is relatively durable, and structures visibly significant inequalities between groups within a given society. In a passage from an early version of *Economy and Society*, which he did not include in later ones, Weber suggests that domination, so understood, can take two very different forms. In the first, it operates through the *commands* which one party gives the other. In the second, it operates through the *control* which the first party exercises over the circumstances in which the second acts.

This is a significant difference. Typically, in one case command evokes obedience. That is, those to whom it is imparted suspend consideration of their own interests and preferences, replacing it with the consideration of the content of the command, and thus of the commander's own interests and preference. In the other case, the subordinate party acts chiefly on the basis of his own preferences; but the fact of acting in a situation where certain strategic resources are monopolized by the other party induces him to comply with that party's superiority. Political power is the obvious example of this first configuration; the second is exemplified by economic power. (Weber mentions the power indirectly exercised on farmers or peasants of a given region by a bank which is the only source of credit to which those farmers or peasants have access.)

Command and obedience

Here, we are interested in political power. Concerning this, Weber asks what are the motivations which typically induce the person who receives the command to obey. And, in the first instance, his answer does not refer to legitimacy. Initially, Weber mentions two motivations of a different kind. In one case the subject obeys the command without expressly deciding to do so: because he has always done so; because he does not even think about the possibility of doing otherwise, of disobeying. As Bagehot says, 'the best security for people doing their duty is that they should know of nothing else to do'. Very often, in the course of prehistory and history, for a given subject – a slave vis-à-vis the master, a child vis-à-vis an adult, or a woman vis-à-vis a man – obedience has constituted straightforward, taken-for-granted aspect of a given subject's existential position.

The other kind of motivation is very different. Here, the command creates a problematical situation, being issued in a context in which the subject has her own preferences, and her own ideas on how to commit her resources, which do not coincide with the content of the command. On this account, the subject is compelled, more or less self-consciously, to deliberate on how to react to the command itself. She compares the advantages and disadvantages of obeying with those of not obeying, the consequences to be feared and those to be hoped for from each alternative, and takes into account the relative probabilities. It is on the basis of this calculation that the subject decides to obey or not to obey.

These two modalities of response to command – one totally routinized and unreflected, and the other highly reflexive – lead up to a third one. Here, obedience takes place, if it does, on the basis of a sense of moral obligation, of what might be called a sense of the '*oughtful-ness*' of obedience. It is to this third modality that the notion of legitimacy applies.

Legitimacy and its limitations

At this point, Weber associates himself with a view often expressed in the history of Western political and social thought, one that Rousseau expressed particularly pointedly: 'The strongest is never strong enough to be always the master, unless he transforms strength into right, and obedience into duty.' When this happens, obedience can more easily induce a subject to sideline his own preferences, and to do so even without a preponderance of favourable calculations over unfavourable ones regarding such obedience. Typically, obedience motivated by a sense of moral obligation is more generous and open-ended than one based on calculations. It is therefore less costly for those who command and sometimes also psychologically less burdensome for those who obey. All things being equal, a political order where such motivations frequently induce compliance with commands – let us call it a *legitimate* political order – can be expected to be more durable, more effective and more secure than one which is not legitimate.

It is at this point that Weber introduces a new and creative argument to the discussion on the advantages of legitimacy, and suggests a distinctive new approach to the ancient topic of the forms of government. Without mentioning it, he elaborates on the position taken by Rousseau. In a political order it is important for those who govern to be able to advance plausible reasons which both justify that command and motivate those under their command to a morally oriented obedience, one inspired by a sense of its 'oughtful-ness'. But, if this is true, Weber holds: *first*, it is important to consider what are the main, typical reasons advanced when asking for obedience (and, if all goes well, are accepted when granting obedience); *second*, given a plurality of political orders with differing responses to the first question, one may ask whether and how they differ regarding other, possibly unrelated, aspects. In other words, polities can be usefully differentiated from one another by asking what kind of legitimacy they possess.

On the basis of these assumptions, Weber develops a whole typology of political orders, characterized by ways in which, within each, commanders typically argue, expressly or implicitly, their right to command and the duty of obedience which lies upon those they command. But the typology does not stop here. Those characteristic ways are presented as constraints, as boundaries imposed on the variable conditions presented by political orders, which also affect other aspects of their structure and their operations.

I speak of 'constraints' here, for various reasons. Weber addresses *in the first place* the diverse nature of the legitimacy of political orders, for this (he feels) is a highly significant variable which previous theorists have not considered deeply enough. But he is far from considering the nature of legitimacy as *the cause* of other significant ways in which those orders differ from one another. Attributing this causal significance to the nature of legitimacy would be an idealistic position, whereas Weber's arguments about politics (even more than about other matters) are grounded in a very realistic viewpoint. This results from the following considerations.

First of all, legitimacy is not an innate, primordial quality of a political order. Typically, a political order acquires its legitimacy in the course of its historical career. Often, at first, it becomes established on factual grounds, by making it clear that those in power are capable of sanctioning their commands by having recourse to violence or the threat of violence. Only subsequently may such a political order acquire a quality of legitimacy – that is, be capable of generating and activating sentiments of morally motivated submission to its commands, and perhaps even sentiments of identification with itself by those who are subject to these commands.

Second: even when a legitimate political order undergoes a crisis of legitimacy, by failing to evoke in the addressees of commands a wilful and dutiful obedience, in the short term it can maintain itself in existence, purely by demonstrating anew its capacity to exercise coercion, or by appealing to other considerations of a factual nature. And that 'short term' need not be *that short*. For instance, according to authoritative contemporary scholars, even though the political regimes imposed by the Soviet Union upon Eastern European countries after the Second World War were constitutionally lacking in legitimacy, they lasted a long time, essentially due to the reasonable fear that if one of those countries attempted to subvert the collectivist regime and to defect from the Soviet bloc, the Soviet army would not hesitate to intervene most punitively.

In the third place, Weber does not suggest that, when it exists, the legitimacy of a political order is necessarily present over the whole span between the top leadership and the rest of society. Legitimacy can still make a political order durable and effective even if it is present only in the beliefs and disposit-ions of a narrow social minority, as long as this comprises the people who are directly involved in the day-to-day management of political and administrative affairs, and who benefit from being so involved.

A Roman emperor is credited with the expression *oderint dum metuant* – I do not mind if they (my subjects) hate me as long as they fear me. This formula is much less dangerous if it inspires the management of power relations with reference to the subjects at large, than if it concerns the administrative apparatus, beginning of course with the praetorian guard. Where this apparatus is concerned, it is important and perhaps indispensable that it should act also on the basis of a sense of loyalty towards the top of the system, acknowledging and enforcing the right to rule of those at the top. It is helpful to reconsider the satellite countries of the Soviet bloc after the Second World War. Very likely, the prolonged tenure in power of its top leadership was due also to the existence of a sizeable minority of individuals who believed in the system, identified with it, and were also committed to it on ideological grounds. Conceivably, rule became untenable when, in the long term, this personnel found itself unable to sustain such commitment.

Furthermore, as Weber understands it, legitimacy should not be considered simply as a resource of the powerful, as something which unconditionally stabilizes and enhances their power. As we shall see, every kind of legitimacy implicitly imposes certain boundaries on domination and makes it unable to undertake certain lines of action (necessary as they may be) without incurring the risk of de-legitimizing itself.

Finally, in Weber's view, the political issue that trumped all others concerned the relations between sovereign states, each seeking to define and assert autonomously its own interests, if necessary through war. Now, sovereign states do not give commands to one another; they do not obey (or disobey) one another. Rather, their reciprocal relations are based on the nature and the entity of their respective might – on their factual ability to block or overpower the resistance or the interference of other states. Thus, where this most significant aspect of the political sphere is concerned, the question of legitimacy simply does not arise.

A typology of legitimacy

So far I have placed the matter of legitimacy in a broader context, and warned the reader against an overestimation of its empirical significance, because in the course of history many significant political commands have been issued and obeyed whether they were legitimate or not. At this point we may align ourselves with conventional readings of Weber. Let us consider, then, his treatment of the types of legitimacy, and of the way in which they relate to other aspects of the political order. Naturally those configurations have varied a great deal historically, but their variety can be both reflected and simplified by a typology. The ideal types below distinguish and contrast just three fundamental patterns.

Traditional legitimacy   Here, what establishes the entitlement to issue commands at one end and the duty to obey them at the other is the appeal to the intrinsic validity and goodness of that which has always been the case. This involves a devotion to a past as far as possible remote, perhaps known only through myth, but considered as the source of every correct understanding of the way people should behave – and if necessary be *made* to behave.

It is duration over time which makes sacred, in the long run, a given way of conceiving reality and of constraining and orienting actions. Thus, command is legitimate when it can plausibly represent itself as the reaffirmation today of obligations and duties which already existed in the past and which, in turn, were backed by the previous era and so on. Typically, whoever commands presents himself as the current representative of a long sequence of forebears who, each in his own time, had exercised command over the forebears of those who are to obey today.

Charismatic legitimacy   Here, we encounter a totally different situation. The commitment to tradition as the ground itself of what is true and right is challenged and subverted by extraordinary forces. These break into the present by expressing themselves through leaders endowed with a 'gift of grace' (charisma). Such a gift manifests itself in unprecedented material or spiritual achievements: military expeditions conducted with unprecedented energy and yielding much booty; the proclamation of new, inspiring truths and of new paths to moral justification and salvation. The leaders capable of those feats issue imperious commands, obedience to which is required in order to accomplish the feats. The obedience of the common people constitutes the homage of believers in the forces the leader embodies, and which through him assert their superiority over all that is routine or traditional.

Legal-rational legitimacy   Of the two types of legitimacy considered so far, the traditional one – in many, highly different variants – is the one most obviously present in history. Charismatic legitimacy is a recurrent but relatively rare phenomenon, forcefully manifesting itself (as we have seen) in unexpected prophets proclaiming 'new heavens and new earths' or in formidable war leaders. Legal-rational legitimacy, in turn, appears in Weber's treatment chiefly as a peculiarity of the modern political experience, and as a component of its central political institution – the state.

Here, typically, particular commands that require obedience are represented as correct instantiations of general ones, and these in turn are represented as specifications of more general commands yet, and so on. The validity of all such commands is grounded in the fact that they have been generated according to norms that authorize certain individuals to issue them, and place various, publicly recognized, constraints on the content commands can take. Thus, obedience is expected, not as homage to the superiority of particular individuals issuing commands, but as dutiful observance of a whole system of norms.

Correlates of legitimacy

Weber holds that the legitimacy with which a political order is endowed is not a self-standing characteristic lacking further consequences and implications; rather, it is systematically associated with other significant aspects of the order itself. Let us consider some of those aspects.

1   In a given political order, how are the summit and the base typically represented? When the order possesses traditional legitimacy, whoever stands at its head represents and justifies himself as a patriarch, as the master and custodian of the population that is subjected to his commands. This population, in turn, is seen as composed of personal dependants and of members of the family of the patriarch. In an order endowed with charismatic legitimacy the top position is held by an individual who is a leader (military or spiritual) and whose exceptional gifts allow him to confer extraordinary benefits to a population seen as made of followers. In an order with legal-rational legitimacy, too, those who hold the top positions appear as the occupants of a role which depersonalizes them, and the population is seen as an ensemble of citizens, of individuals who are in principle equal one to another.

2   A recurring function of political orders consists of the formation and enforcement of judicial verdicts sanctioning the non-observance of the rules of conduct of the collectivity through judicial judgments. In orders with traditional legitimacy the verdicts typically appeal to a rule held to exist from time immemorial, and which the judge 'finds'. In those with charismatic legitimacy verdicts do not refer to a pre-existent rule, but express either directly, or through followers whom the leader trusts, his own unchallengeable will. In legal-rational orders the production of verdicts is highly discursive, being grounded in principle on the so-called judicial syllogism. This states a general rule, which is valid because properly formed, ascertains certain factual circumstances and applies the rule to the circumstances.

3   How does a political order provision itself with economic resources in order to fund its own activities? Generally, in an order with traditional legitimacy, it is not possible to distinguish between the personal resources of the head of the order and those vested in the order itself. Thus, political activities are funded from the personal resources of the chief, perhaps supplemented by tributes through which members of the collectivity express their own subjection. An order with charismatic legitimacy is funded chiefly by the booty produced by the leader's military successes, or on

the basis of occasional exactions or 'gifts' which manifest the followers' gratitude and loyalty. In an order with legal-rational legitimacy it is possible to distinguish clearly between the 'private' resources of common individuals and of those who are charged with political responsibilities, and the public resources which belong to the order itself. These are continually replenished through regular and predictable levies, especially taxes and imposts.

4 To what recurrent problems are political orders exposed on account of the legitimacy that characterizes them? Those with traditional legitimacy may be unable to respond promptly and effectively to new dangers and opportunities by taking initiatives which are not underwritten by tradition. Generally, they confront this danger by juxtaposing some activities based on the discretion of the powerful (perhaps masked by an appeal to ancient precedents which had been 'forgotten') to the traditional activities, adequate for recurrent and routinized circumstances. But such innovations present their own danger. If they occur too frequently they can erode the sense of the sacredness of the past on which the legitimacy itself rests. Typically, a charismatically legitimated order encounters the following problem: it must repeatedly justify itself and acquire new resources by means of new initiatives and achievements, particularly of a military and economic nature, in order to renew the followers' trust in the extraordinary qualities of the leader. But the more the leader responds to this need, the greater the probability of his fall. Furthermore, it is difficult for an order that depends expressly on the exceptional qualities of a given individual to ensure its continuity once that individual leaves the scene. Neither this problem, nor that of justifying unprecedented political action, are so acute for political orders with legal-rational legitimacy. These, however, encounter a different problem, signalled not so much in Weber's own writings as in those by Carl Schmitt and Habermas, namely, how to confer authentic moral resonance in the minds of citizens to commands, both general and particular, which are deemed valid exclusively because certain formal procedures have been followed in producing them. Such procedures do not appeal to other shared values than

those of the 'rules of the game', for they confer only *legality* on commands – a rather hollow value.

The day-to-day dimension of politics and the role of the staff

We have seen some ways in which Weber conceptually differentiates the phenomenon of political domination, by connecting various aspects of it, from judicial to fiscal ones, to the typology of legitimation. But there is a further aspect to which Weber attached the greatest importance. Many conventional comparisons between political orders paid attention chiefly to the ways in which they were structured at the top, as in the distinction between monarchy, aristocracy and democracy, or to the ways major policies were formed, as in the distinction between parliamentary and presidential democracies. They neglected to consider a phenomenon common to all political orders, which Weber discussed extensively, both in his scholarly writings and in those commenting on current political affairs.

There exists within each political order, immediately below the top level, what he called its *staff* – a relatively large number of people who are (at any rate formally) at the service of that summit. They keep it informed of the needs of the collectivity; see to it that those needs are met on a day-to-day basis; extract from the economy the resources necessary for funding policies; assist in the formation and implementation of those policies; and so on. Whatever the constitutional arrangements empowering an order and limiting its powers, it is the staff who are in charge of administration, that is, of the day-to-day dimension of politics, where the policies deliberated at the top are (or are not!) brought to bear on a country's existence.

This theme was of great interest to Weber, first, because in his opinion and that of others, in Wilhelmine Germany the relationship between the political summit and the administrative staff had not been properly settled. Neither the parliamentary institutions of the empire nor the cabinet could effectively steer the political system as a whole, to counterbalance the power which had been accumulating, de jure or de facto, in the bureaucratic apparatus, beginning with its military component. After the German defeat in the Great War there was a danger that this imbalance could reproduce itself in the republican regime, if the newly established parliamentary system did not manage to produce an adequate leadership.

A further reason for Weber's interest in this topic was probably that he intended to develop an expressly sociological theory of the workings of polities, countering those juridical theories which privileged their constitutional and political aspects, while neglecting the significance of administrative structures and practices, that is, of what we might call the interface between a country's politics and its other activities.

The relationship between the political centre and the staff

Weber's distinctive emphasis on administrative structures and practices led to a focus on one major, recurrent problem. Although key political decisions are formed at a country's capital, or in a small number of major centres, the administrative action to implement them must often take place at the periphery. Frequently, this implementation is conducted in a way that maximizes the autonomy and the material and status privileges of the administrative personnel. In turn, this necessarily reduces the leverage which the political centre can effectively exercise on the country as a whole, particularly its hold on the country's resources. For this reason, Weber insisted, one must pay attention to the ways in which a polity structures its administrative staff.

In confronting this topic, Weber made some of his most significant sociological contributions, by formulating typologies aimed at questions such as the following. Who, in a polity, assists those occupying the top positions in forming decisions, and in determining the content of policies? What arrangements are made to implement those policies on a day-by-day basis, throughout the territory the polity controls? What kind of personnel manages these arrangements, how is it selected, deployed and rewarded? And how is its conduct monitored?

Once more, the answers to these questions vary, according to Weber, depending on the legitimacy characterizing the polity. To simplify his complex elaboration of those answers, I will quote a passage from Machiavelli's *Prince* (1532), relating (in Weber's own vocabulary) to polities with traditional legitimation:

> Those principalities of which one knows find themselves governed in two different manners. Either by on the one hand the prince, and on the other only servants, who by the prince's grace and favour assist him in governing in the capacity of ministers. Or by the prince and barons, who hold such positions not from the lord's grace, but from the antiquity of their blood. (1940: 15)

Without referring to Machiavelli, Weber suggests that administrative arrangements of the first type elaborate and expand the relationship between a master and his domestic subordinates, in particular those entrusted with the management of the master's possessions. Their social status is drastically inferior to that of the lord: they depend completely on his favour, being supported by him either directly, as components of his family and members of his household, or indirectly, when the lord allows them to avail themselves of some of the revenues produced by their performance of administrative, fiscal or other activities on the master's behalf.

Barons, on the contrary, enjoy an honourable social status, relatively similar to that of the lord. They establish relations with him which have a distinctive hierarchical character, and commit themselves to serving him. But those relations rest on their consent, which is at least partially negotiated. Thus their service to the lord does not have a demeaning character and does not entail total inferiority. Even if the lord assigns resources to the barons – typically, grants them a fief – conceptually this arrangement respects the social identity of the baron. He is in the first place a warrior; as such, and as the leader of his own dependants, he is to some extent a 'peer' of the lord himself.

Both types of political administrative personnel – serfs and barons – have one tendency in common. As far as they can, they treat the resources assigned for tasks they are to perform for the lord as their own resources, as part of their patrimony. To the extent that they succeed (at first purely de facto, later perhaps de jure), the lord's control over the uses of those resources is of course diminished. Thus, lords typically resist that tendency, but often cannot stop a kind of entropic process. The polity becomes progressively disarticulated and can less and less be controlled from the centre as a whole.

In charismatically legitimated polities, the leader freely chooses those who are going to collaborate with him from those who have been the first to spontaneously recognize his extraordinary qualities and commit themselves to following him. As a result, according to Weber:

> The administrative staff of a charismatic leader does not consist of 'officials'; least of all are its members technically trained. It is not chosen on the basis of social privilege nor from the point of view of domestic or personal dependency. It is rather chosen in terms of the charismatic qualities of its members. The prophet has his disciples; the warlord his body-guard; the leader, generally, his agents (*Vertrauensmänner*). There is no such thing as appointment or dismissal, no career, no promotion. There is only a call at the instance of the leader on the basis of the charismatic qualifications of those he summons. There is no hierarchy; the leader merely intervenes in general or individual cases when he considers the members of his staff lacking in charismatic qualification for a given task. There is no such thing as a bailiwick or definite sphere of competence, and no appropriation of official powers on the basis of social privileges . . . There is no such thing as a salary or a benefice. (1978: 243)

In charismatically legitimate polities, the members of the staff are not chiefly concerned with how to increase their margins of independence with respect to the leader, but rather with how to stabilize their own advantageous position. In particular, this is threatened by the leader's mortality, and by the possibility of failure in some of the initiatives he takes in order to give renewed proof that his charisma persists. To secure themselves against those contingencies, such polities tend to institutionalize charisma itself, generally by fashioning arrangements which make it transmissible, or by vesting aspects of it in the holding of a particular office.

Finally, in polities with legal-rational legitimacy, the staff is recruited and organized according to a model that Weber, following established usage, calls bureaucratic. His analysis of bureaucracy constitutes one of the most significant contributions to social theory and as such it deserves to be discussed more widely in the context of a related theme that was also of great importance to Weber: the nature of the modern state. This is our concern in the final chapter.

7
The State and Bureaucracy

Modernity of the state

For Weber, the expressions 'state' and 'modern state' have basically the same meaning. While some passages in his writings may suggest otherwise, according to Weber, political orders to which the label 'state' is appropriate first appeared on the historical scene in early-modern Europe, though state-like ways of building and managing political power have occurred in earlier epochs and in other parts of the world.

The historical particularity of the state stems from two considerations. First, the earliest historical appearances of the state were not sudden events, but were the result of a complex and original elaboration of previous political arrangements, which have left their own imprint on the state itself. Two of these arrangements, according to Weber, were themselves peculiar to the late-medieval, early-modern phase of European history: the distinctive, 'Western' variant of feudalism (a phenomenon which also appears elsewhere), and the so-called *Ständestaat* or 'polity of the estates', which is, itself, exclusively a European phenomenon.

In the second place, Weber also considers the state to be one manifestation among others (although a particularly significant one) of a wider historical particularity of the West, particularly evident in modernity. As discussed in chapter 3, the West has undertaken the rationalization of multiple social and cultural phenomena in a peculiarly demanding and self-conscious manner. These, in their rationalized form, have developed a powerfully expansive dynamic, and have supplanted or marginalized those different ways of confronting similar tasks which other civilizations and cultures had previously practised.

The state in a sociological perspective

Despite his intentions, Weber was not able to write a *Staatssoziologie*. His writings on this subject are not extensive, much less systematic, and do not convey the importance attributed by him to this theme, from both an intellectual and a personal viewpoint. Furthermore, much of his writing on this subject was part of the German intellectual patrimony of his time, and only our scant familiarity with that patrimony makes us unaware that, significant as they may be, some of his statements on the state were not particularly original. Perhaps the projected *Staatssoziologie* was intended to add to the existing knowledge regarding the state, which chiefly reflected the perspectives of legal and historical scholarship.

The few things Weber says concerning his specifically sociological way of discussing the state (as other social realities) seek to differentiate sociological discourse from that of those two disciplines, law and history. It has been said that there is an Anglo-Saxon way of conceiving the state *as a convenience* and a German way of conceiving it *as an entity*. In fact, in Wilhelmine Germany, both the historical and the legal discourses presupposed, or elaborated, this second conception. Within it, the state appears as something entirely separate from the lines of individuals, forming an entity which operates according to its own logic, with its own ethical justification and historical mission.

Sociological discourse, as Weber conceived and practised it, was bound to differ from and to challenge such a way of understanding the state (or, for that matter other collective realities), attributing to it a unitary identity and a unitary will that transcends those of the individuals it comprises. As I have argued with reference to the *Stände*, every collective reality exists in so far as a plurality of individuals is traversed by commonalities in the subjective processes through which those individuals perceive and evaluate their situation. Such commonalities engender relatively stable dispositions of united action towards shared material and ideal interests.

This conception is also appropriate when discussing the state. According to Weber, the state exists *if and in so far as*, within a relatively wide and durable plurality of individuals, the activities involving political power (in terms of both those who hold power and those who are subject to it) assume a certain configuration. Thus, in principle, *state-ness* (as we have labelled it) is not a quality that a political body categorically possesses or does not possess, once and for all – it is a variable. The state exists to the extent that the political activities affecting a delimited but relatively large territory are conducted in certain ways by personnel selected and activated through certain practices, and that these political activities address a relatively wide domain of social interests, and acquire and deploy economic resources in a relatively predictable and orderly manner. In turn, this requires that the action generated by innumerable individuals should reflect consistently those specific patterns of political activity.

Thus, Weber criticizes (one is tempted to say 'unmasks') the German tendency to theorize the state as a self-standing reality. Instead, he construes it as the continuously reproduced result of the convergence of innumerable lines of individual activity. However, he concedes three justifications to that tendency. First, it has some validity in the context of legal discourse, for this adopts an expressly normative posture towards social reality, rather than one that is empirically grounded (such as sociological discourse). Second, in the context of sociological discourse, employing potentially reifying expressions such as 'the state', rather than recalling explicitly its individual and subjective makings, assists in streamlining the argument.

The third consideration deserves particular attention because it reveals the depth and complexity of Weber's thought, although here I phrase it somewhat roughly. 'The state' as a superior entity, as the protagonist of history, is a myth. It is, however, a myth that enjoys strong, uncritical credence in some people (and here one senses that Weber is thinking of the intense commitment of higher officials to the mission of a particular bureaucratic apparatus, such as the

Prussian one). This very credence impinges significantly on such people's conduct, rendering it specifically and consistently 'state-like'.

There are two considerations concerning this last point. First, we may connect it with Weber's philosophical anthropology (mentioned in chapter 2). Human beings attach intrinsically arbitrary meanings to reality, but must conceal such arbitrariness from themselves, for the awareness of it would weaken and deprive those meanings of effectiveness. The second consideration is suggested by something I often hear in Italian public (and private!) discourse: 'We Italians do not have *il senso dello stato*.' What makes this frequent comment plausible (alas) is that often, in Italy, laws which are inspired by a relatively strong concept of 'the state', and which are intended to orient and discipline the conduct of politicians, public officials and citizens, do not call forth authentically 'state-like' flows of activities from them. The subjective processes that actually take place in their minds do not conform with those laws, and thus do not induce them to conduct themselves as 'proper' politicians, public officials or citizens. Many centuries ago, Dante said it all: 'The laws are there, but who puts himself behind them?' Put otherwise, law-in-the-statutes fails to become law-in-action.

After looking at the main differences between the 'discourse on the state' expressed by Weber's contemporaries, and Weber's own, let us consider some substantial aspects of the latter, in order to avoid a misunderstanding of its method. If, as we said, the state exists if and in so far as innumerable individuals act in certain ways in certain aspects of their existence, these ways in turn typically form the content of publicly promulgated, sanctioned expectations: they form complexes of practices made possible and enjoined by certain material and intellectual resources, and are part of a pre-structured institutional context.

This holds for Weber as much as for Marx, who formulated this intuition in a memorable passage of *The Eighteenth Brumaire of Louis Bonaparte*: 'Men make their own history, but they do not make it just as they please; they do not make it under circumstances chosen by themselves, but under circumstances directly found, given and transmitted from the past' (quoted from *The Marx–Engels Reader*, edited by Robert

C. Tucker (New York: Norton, 1972): 437). Although that text of Marx's had an expressly political theme, his thought generally privileged the economic aspect of the socio-historical process, thus the means and the relations of production, and the ways in which these conditioned the actions of individuals. As we know, aware as he was of the significance of that aspect, Weber was at least as aware of the significance of others, beginning with the political aspect.

In the context of modernity, then, what constraints on the actions of individuals and groups derive from the existence of a political entity that one may appropriately call a state? What alternatives does it open or foreclose to that action, what interests does it favour or disfavour, what problems does it solve or create? In other words, what species of political animal *is* the state?

Nature of the state

We have already suggested some answers in considering Weber's typology of political domination. Let us review them:

- at the core of the institutional identity of the state, *qua* political entity, lies organized violence. The state, furthermore, monopolizes this means to the domination of people over people;
- the state differs from other forms of political domination (among other things) by possessing legal-rational legitimacy. That is, law plays a critical role in determining its legitimacy (which – as we have seen – has its limitations, for it tends to reduce everything to mere legality);
- the state provisions itself with economic resources chiefly via taxation;
- those individuals who are the object of the state's domination appear more and more as citizens, that is, as individuals endowed with a subjectivity which the state acknowledges and safeguards. Taken altogether, they constitute a new kind of political community – a nation;
- the administrative arrangements entrusted with the implementation of the state's policies are bureaucratic in nature. (We shall say more on this shortly.)

To broaden and complement these answers, let us consider a relatively extensive definition of the (modern) state given by Weber:

> The primary formal characteristics of the modern state are as follows: It possesses an administrative order subject to change by legislation, to which the organized activities of the administrative staff, which are also controlled by legislation, are oriented. This system of order claims binding authority not only over the members of the state, the citizens, most of whom have obtained membership by birth, but also to a very large extent over all action taking place in the area of its jurisdiction. It is thus a compulsory organization with a territorial basis. Furthermore, today, the use of force is regarded as legitimate only so far as it is either permitted by the state or prescribed by it. . . The claim of the modern state to monopolize the use of force is as essential to it as its character of compulsory jurisdiction and of continuous operation. (Weber 1978: 56)

This definition, together with other passages from Weber's writings, allows us to complete our conceptual portrait of the state. In particular: the state is an ensemble of practices, facilities and faculties of rule, personnel, etc., which, although large, complex and internally diversified, represents itself as *one* entity. The above definition suggests this by speaking of the state's monopoly of organized violence – for a monopoly implies a single centre of control and initiative – and by referring to the territory on which the state affirms the exclusivity of its own jurisdiction.

What the state *does*, and in particular to what ends it addresses its activities, is a very significant question, but not one allowing for an answer that is valid for all states in all situations. Put otherwise, the state's activities are intrinsically contingent; the set of ends they pursue is open-ended. In the above definition, this results from the fact that it assigns to legislation the task of changing the content of a state's administrative and juridical order, and of determining the content of its administrative activities. Some passages from *Economy and Society,* and a particularly emphatic one from *Politics as a Vocation,* insist on this point. It is not possible to determine conceptually the ends of state action, for empirically these vary a great deal from one situation to another.

This is also the conclusion that results from Weber's positivistic view of law, and from the repeated reference to statutory legislation in his writings. In that view, law is constituted by all decisions taken by the state which follow certain formal procedures, but which do not necessarily reflect any substantive principle governing the law's content. (Hence, once more, the awkward relationship between legitimacy and legality.) Furthermore, in the liberal-democratic state the very existence of competing parties, each seeking to assert a different programme and establish a different leadership emphasizes the contingent nature of these two vital aspects of the state.

Typical modalities of state action

Typically, state action is rationally oriented. This develops from the actual nature of its legitimacy, and finds expression in various aspects of its political and administrative institutions. These are primarily conceived and established through constitutional and organizational decisions which are to a considerable extent self-conscious and explicit. By the same token they are subject to revision by means of legislation, often reflecting shifts in the power relations between parties. Furthermore, in principle those institutions operate in such a way as to maximize rationality, that is: they expressly consider the means and ends appropriate to expressly ascertained circumstances; they aim to optimize the relationship between the employment of means and the attainment of ends; they are disposed, if necessary, to revise or suspend existing arrangements and practices and to replace them with others; and, as far as possible, through deliberate programming they seek to render their own activities (and those of other subjects affected by them) predictable in their modalities, costs, risks and outcomes.

In Weber, this emphasis on the rational character of the state distances his views from many commonplace understandings and critiques; it is accompanied by a sharp sense of the limitations and paradoxes of rationality in the political sphere in general, and in the state in particular. First, the choice of rationality as the standard and the guide of action is not in itself rational. Second, that choice entails costs, beginning with the suppression or marginalization of incompatible values, and creates problems of its own. Third, the political sphere revolves around a particular form of power, grounded in violence. This subjects it to an inevitable *quantum* of irrationality, particularly apparent in the irreducible contingency of the outcomes of an armed conflict.

Furthermore, this irrational element is emphasized by a central characteristic of the modern political universe – the plurality of the states which inhabit it and form it. Weber's sociological writings do not emphasize that characteristic, perhaps because they take it for granted. In the definition quoted on page 110, however, the reference to a territory as the ambit of a state's action implies that each state is juxtaposed to others, each with a different territorial base.

Now, the relations between coexisting states are not managed through their shared subordination to a higher political entity standing over all of them, and authorizing or regulating activities, by exercising its own jurisdiction on them. Instead, each state can and must define autonomously its own vital interests, and assert them over the contrasting ones of other states by engaging in armed violence, unless that contrast can be otherwise mediated or moderated.

Without dwelling on the topic at length, Weber clearly suggests all this in a lively public and scholarly debate of the time, concerning so-called *Machtpolitik* – power politics – and in particular the historical role of the 'great powers'. It is also suggested by an expression inspired by the writing of Thucydides, 'politisches Pragma', which I would freely translate as follows: in politics, when all is said and done, it's facts that matter.

But 'facts', in the political sphere, are multiple and variable; they need to be ascertained and evaluated, and can change rapidly, partly because in pursuing its own interest each state can ally itself with others, and in this way modify the circumstances. This imparts to state action a further characteristic – its dynamic character. Each state is disposed to undertake policies intended to increase its own might, that is, its capacity to realize its own interests in spite of their contrast with those of other states.

The ancient concept of *raison d'état* already implies this. The 'reason' in question is formal in nature, and its concrete content can vary in different circumstances. In the course of political modernization, however, the interests which the 'reason of state' is supposed to realize are generally seen as those of a historically new political subject, the nation. This is a particularly inclusive and durable political community, whose growing salience both limits and justifies the diverse inequalities between the summit and the base which all forms of political domination entail.

Weber acknowledges that it is difficult to generalize regarding the commonalities in which a nation grounds its identity. Yet, however constituted, each nation has interests of its own, which it is the task of the state to advance politically. On this account, Weber dissents from views that extol *Machtpolitik* for its own sake, and that favour the exemption of the state from identifying and pursuing national interests, authorizing it instead to increase continuously its might as an end in itself.

At the time Weber wrote, the constitutional arrangements of the state were liberal-democratic in nature. As such, they shaped the state as an ensemble of organs with different competences and tasks, expressly assigned to them by constitutional or normal legislation. Furthermore, this established and protected various individual rights, such as the right of property, the right to form and express opinions and so forth. Such arrangements allowed the social base of the state – the national population – to peaceably and regularly affect the composition of state organs, beginning with legislatures, via the open and free competition between parties for popular support.

Genesis and development of the state

In Weber's sociological writings, this ideal-typical portrait of the state is complemented by two main treatments of its genesis. *Economy and Society* describes a sequence of ideal types representing successive approximations to the contemporary liberaldemocratic state: in particular, the feudal system of rule, the *Ständestaat*, absolutism. Here, however, I refer chiefly to *Politics as a Vocation*, where the same historical material is presented from a narrative rather than a conceptual perspective.

Interestingly, this text frames its account of the genesis of the state by analogy with the Marxist rendering of the genesis of modern capitalism. Marx had emphasized the expropriation of the means of production at the hands of the bourgeoisie. Weber argues that the state has developed through a similar process. Here, a sovereign centre originally controlled by a princely dynasty progressively expropriates facilities and faculties of rule that were previously vested in a plurality of relatively autonomous, self-activating subjects, such as: feudal lords; the assembly of the estates of a given region; tax farmers; colonels who on their own initiative, and for their own profit (if successful) organized, equipped and funded military regiments; notables who exercised policing and jurisdictional prerogatives over a region; and so forth.

Early on, and at their own behest, those varied subjects undertook a range of political-administrative activities on behalf of the larger polity, committing their own resources for their own advantage (economic or status advantage). Subsequently, the same activities were entrusted instead to organs expressly charged with them, and which had been intentionally established for the systematic and continuous conduct of more or less specialized activities. Such organs were funded from the public purse. They operated on the basis of express constitutional and legislative norms, or of directives duly issued by higher organs, and they recruited their personnel on the basis of established procedures. The members of some organs were elected by narrower or wider constituencies; those of others were selected through open competitions intended to verify objectively the qualifications of applicants. Among those qualifications, this selection process increasingly emphasized the applicants' possession of appropriate specialized, expert knowledge.

In the process, the institutional basis for the performance of political or administrative tasks (including judicial, military, fiscal and police tasks) ceases to be the *right* to perform them that was previously vested in some individual or bodies. It becomes the *duty* to perform them, attached to the holding of diverse offices by diverse people, all of whom, however, are supposed in principle to serve not their own interest, but the public interest.

It is assumed to be in the public interest, say, that judicial verdicts be more and more rationally justified, by referring to bodies of literate, *taught and learned* law; that the economic resources necessary for funding all state activities be 'extracted' from the economy in a more and more predictable and efficient manner; that armies and navies be so equipped and officered as to turn them into more and more effective instruments of organized violence, capable of confronting the enemies' challenge. It is in order to observe this preference that the political centre confiscates relevant faculties and facilities of rule from their traditional holders, and vests them, as already indicated, in new holders. Typically, these have been expressly trained for such employment, and in practising the related activities are expected to set aside their own personal concerns. Their activities are to be controlled, instead, by their knowledge, beginning with the knowledge of norms and other public directives. These, in turn, are expected to articulate and specify the highest, most general commands, those issued by the sovereign and her councils.

In fact, this statement should not be taken too literally. Often, in the process of state-making the institutional and material facilities relevant to political tasks, and vested in traditional holders, were not so much confiscated as sidestepped by the development of new resources that only the political centre could accumulate and manage. For instance, the law taught in universities is more relevant to the requirements and the potentialities of the growing markets and of city life than vernacular law; but for a while vernacular bodies of custom, sanctioned by landowners, remained effective in the countryside. The revenues levied by specialized fiscal offices turned out to be greater, more calculable, and more compatible with growing commercial economies than the exactions in goods and services which local lords continued to practise (for instance, by monopolizing the mills).

Finally, only standing armies funded from those revenues, and, fielded on behalf of the ruler, can avail themselves of the new material and social technologies for waging war – new types of fortification, artillery, the intense and assiduous training and the systematic provisioning and barracking of troops. It is of little significance whether or not local lords continue to maintain troops led by them and formed by their own dependants, or whether communities continue to commandeer local militias.

Whatever the paths followed in this momentous transition, it has one general import: the growing rationalization of the political sphere. Essentially, the new arrangements render the political management and the administration of the territory more uniform, more subject to planning and to coordination, and thus more predictable. Furthermore, economies of scale become possible – consider the advantages of having just a few factories produce all the ordnance, or all the uniforms, for a larger and larger army. Also, more and more exacting forms of discipline in the compliance with the commands and directives of higher officials become possible. (Weber is very aware of the importance of discipline, in the political as well as the economic and religious spheres.) Above all, the new arrangements are made possible by, and in turn make possible, the appeal to new *savoirs*, and thus of new professions.

Political professions

In *Politics as a Vocation* (*Politik als Beruf*) the narrative we have just summarized in the previous section intersects with an argument concerning the professions that are involved in the making and development of modern politics and administration.

As discussed in chapter 4, the concept of *Beruf* holds a central role in *The Protestant Ethic*. Here the entrepreneur's calling appears as a particular embodiment of worldly asceticism, characterized by a direct and assiduous commitment to the increase of capital through profit. More generally, in any calling the daily practice of one's mundane tasks constitutes an occasion for proving one's moral worth and perhaps ascertaining one's spiritual standing. That concept occupies an even more central role in two much later texts of Weber's, both presented as speeches in Munich: respectively, on science (November, 1917), and on politics (February, 1919). This latter text associates the Marx-like theme of expropriation with a treatment of questions which may be formulated, perhaps a bit simplistically, as follows: What is the profession of those who promote the expropriation process? To what profession do those being targeted by this process belong? To what profession do those who advance the process belong? At the end of that process, what professions are entrusted with the conduct of political and administrative affairs?

Coming to terms with these questions involves, in the first place, recognizing that the term 'profession' covers more than one meaning. Furthermore, *Beruf* can be translated into English as occupation *or* profession *or* vocation *or* calling. Each translation points to a different way in which a person can relate to worldly tasks, which in turn can vary from those of a slave to those of a businessman, a doctor, a journalist, a rentier, an artisan, an accountant and so forth.

As far as political and administrative activities are concerned, since the Middle Ages Western experience has presented two fundamental types of protagonist. On the one hand, there are individuals for whom those activities constitute an aspect (mostly honourable, sometimes onerous, more often profitable) of a broader social position, generally a privileged one. Typically, such individuals do not identify closely with those activities, are not expressly trained and qualified for them, and do not make a particularly strong commitment to them.

On the other hand, we encounter individuals for whom political and administrative concerns lie at the centre of their life, and constitute the most significant way of positioning themselves in society, or of orienting and in a sense justifying their very existence. Essentially, the process of state-building, as *Politics as a Vocation* construes it, involves the progressive devaluing of the first type – let us call it the 'notable' – to the advantage of the second, to which we might attach the label 'professional' in the sense in which it is often applied to soldiers, judges, administrators, politicians and so forth.

Of course, state-building is a complex and protracted process, and differs in concrete terms from one situation to another. In particular, the appearance of political parties signals that the process is fairly advanced, since these are generally built and managed by professional politicians whose aim is to promote their professional achievements, albeit with varying degrees of success. Yet, even among modern parties, there have been, and to some extent still are, some which could be labelled 'parties of notables' and which represent the persistence of the first of those two types. In a certain phase of nineteenth-century French history, ironic reference was made to 'the republic of dukes', given the relatively high number of aristocrats holding seats in elected assemblies. A century later, it was Margaret Thatcher, who definitively displaced the aristocratic elements from most of the leading positions in the British Conservative Party. However, at the beginning of the twenty-first century, the link between positions of generalized, but especially economic, social advantage and access to public offices, particularly elective ones, seems to have regained significance and visibility in many countries. Individuals seeking such offices have some probability of success only if they command vast financial resources. This places at an advantage those who can mobilize their own resources, whether personal or corporate, when they first enter the competition. This holds true especially – but alas not exclusively – for the United States.

Despite variations over time and place, the expropriation of the political and administrative prerogatives formerly enjoyed by all types of notable is an inexorable process. In its early phases it is initiated by the princes' interest in acquiring control over the apparatus of rule, by employing individuals who have no proprietary rights in the facilities and faculties of rule they administrate. Later, however, it developed due to the democratization of politics, which initially involves limiting the powers of rulers by transferring some of their power to elective bodies. But it also involves a demand that access to positions in the administrative system (including the judiciary and the military) must depend exclusively on the possession of scholastic and academic credentials, proven by success in competitive examinations. Only this can neutralize the tendency for acquisition of political and administrative positions to be based on ascriptive criteria, while also guaranteeing that objectively validated skills are employed to perform these tasks. The same criterion, of course, must be applied in the promotion of individuals to more significant political and administrative positions.

In response to both democratic and functional requirements, political and administrative facilities and faculties that were previously in the hands of notables are progressively assigned, within the state, to a complex of agencies, or divisions, operating on behalf of the political centre, while being monitored and held accountable by it. In some texts, Weber designates such a complex as *Betrieb*, 'establishment' – an expression which (significantly) is also used for the complex of material and other resources organized by and operating on behalf of a commercial or industrial enterprise. The political-administrative *Betrieb* is typically a large and internally differentiated system, which operates continuously and in a plurality of locales in order to meet varied and changing contingencies. In spite of this, it is unified by its concern with the public interest, by its monopoly over expressly political resources (following Norbert Elias, we can set the state's fiscal monopoly next to its monopoly of organized violence), and by its tendency to rationalize the employment of those resources in the pursuit of that interest.

All of this can take place only through the coordinated activities of innumerable individuals, whose identification with a determinate *Beruf* empowers and orients their action. In other words, in the state as in the capitalist enterprise, *Beruf* systematically interacts with *Betrieb*, the first chiefly pointing to subjective processes, and the second to the objective integration between diverse resources.

Politics and administration

The multiplicity and diversity of the *Berufe* involved in the operations of the state can be reduced to a basic duality, that between politics and administration. The former, in the conventional understanding, produces policies; the latter sees to their implementation.

Originally, at the top, policy-making was the responsibility of a leader – typically the head of a princely dynasty – who sought to expand the territory where he could assert his authority over magnates (Machiavelli's 'barons') and various collective subjects, each with its own constituency, in a region or in a particular trade. Later, under constitutional, and especially under liberal then liberal-democratic regimes, such powers appear to become more symbolic, with the prince or sovereign acting as a figurehead to represent the unity, legitimacy and continuity of the state.

The central political *Beruf*, involved in the making of political choices, the formation of public opinion and the guidance of the state apparatus, comes to be held by the leader of a party – the 'modern prince', in Gramsci's words. A basic difference between such a leader and the sovereign of old, however, is that there are *at least* two parties – each competing for popular consensus and investiture, in order to realize their own distinctive policies.

Furthermore, a modern political party is itself a complex organization, with multiple components relating to different functions or to different sections of the territory. All these parts must in turn have leaders. These compete over formation of the party's platform and over the content of its policies when in power, but above all over the staffing of the party's agencies and, if possible, over the functions and staffing of state agencies. Intra-party competition mostly takes place by advancing different understandings of the party's mission and of its optimal strategy for gaining power and for making use of it when in government. This competition can be quite fierce, for its outcome determines how these questions are settled. Ideally, that outcome identifies the individual who is most suited for leading the party as a whole. By the same token it rewards that person's followers, and in particular its staff, thus linking the top of the party with its rank-and-file.

Under modern conditions, the second kind of political *Beruf* is that of the bureaucrat or administrator. Here, again, we encounter great diversity, for the state's administration represents a vast and complex division of labour. Thus, it harbours a great number of differentiated and coordinated positions, each requiring a different body of knowledge from its functionaries, concerning on the one hand the principles and techniques of correct administrative activity, and on the other the factual conditions on which that activity must bring to bear the directives issuing (directly or indirectly) from the political centre.

Taken as a whole, the state's administrative apparatus must commit all the different experts who form its personnel to achieving the policies decided by the political leaders, who have been invested with that responsibility by the electorate, and are accountable to it. Such experts are as varied as those of the army or the navy official, the officer of the Inland Revenue service, and so on. The apparatus has a hierarchy of its own, and those occupying the higher positions supposedly do so by virtue of superior professional competence. They, too, are functionaries, and as such they are not supposed to orient their own activities according to their own judgement of the merits of official policies, for they bear no responsibility for them. Instead, they should seek to implement them in as impartial and competent a way as possible, conceiving their task as a technical one.

On the one hand, then, the ethical substance of the first *Beruf*, that of properly political personnel, lies in the responsibility they must assume not just for the content of their policies, but for their outcomes under the existing circumstances (which often involve confrontation with opposing interests). The ethical substance of the second *Beruf*, instead, lies in the functionary's willingness to place all his own 'science and conscience' at the service of policies resulting from other people's choices.

This sharp contrast between the two central *Berufe* of the modern political sphere is of course ideal-typical; in an abstract, coherent manner it represents a concrete reality, primarily that of the Wilhelmine Reich, where, as Weber knew, the relationship between politics and administration had always been problematical. He also knew the causes of this; and those causes affected other realities, too.

First, the institutional design of a given political order can, in principle, moderate the contrast between the formation and the execution of policies. In Wilhelmine Germany, for instance, the Kaiser sought to play a political role, particularly through his powers of appointment (for example, he chose the Chancellor) and in matters relating to the military establishment; but he bore no responsibility for those choices. This, together with the weakness of representative institutions (and of parties), generated a kind of political vacuum, where the top layers of the administrative system (still staffed largely by Junker elements, with their authoritarian leanings) hugely increased their own discretion and, de facto, decided policies, while remaining free from responsibility for them.

Second, in Germany, as elsewhere, the state had been taking on more tasks of societal management, which it handed over to its own administrative apparatus. Thus, the effective centre of political life had shifted from the legislature to the executive. This, in turn, was increasingly dependent on its administrative apparatus, for the technical component of the activities of political and administrative organizations had become much more complex and open to innovation. Only professional bureaucrats (if anybody) possessed the requisite knowledge, and capacity to determine the actual content of policies, which were sometimes at variance with the proclaimed aims of official policies.

We have already glimpsed a further phenomenon which rendered problematical the relations between political and administrative personnel. In liberal-democratic regimes the parties compete to form the state's leadership and to decide its policies, but these had become more complex organizations with increasing dependency on the professional expertise of their own functionaries. Of course, for their own legitimation, these appealed to the ideology of the party and to the fact of having been chosen by the party leaders. But, in performing their tasks they, too, sought more or less self-consciously to increase their own autonomy with respect to the leaders themselves. Above all, they advanced (more or less openly) policies that gave top priority to the party's organizational strength and stability, sometimes detracting from its political mission and official programme.

After all, while the properly political leadership of parties was composed at least partly of people who – as Weber wrote – lived *for* politics, their organizational machinery was largely built and managed by people who lived instead *from* politics. These inevitably (though often not self-consciously) understood and performed their own professional tasks in the light of their economic interests, including the interest in making a career within that machinery. Thus, ensuring the continuation of that machinery was their overriding concern, rather than pursuing its official goals, if that pursuit endangered or weakened the machinery.

In sum, according to Weber, the very fact that administration constitutes the day-to-day dimension of politics, and the aspect of it that specifically interfaces with society, creates a measure of opposition between it and the state's properly political leadership. Initially, administrators had assisted the sovereign in expropriating the faculties and facilities of rule originally held by magnates, estate bodies or local notables, who had negotiated the nature of their political contributions with the sovereign, but the new administrative personnel had made those faculties and facilities its own, although formally it handled them not as a matter of right but as a matter of duty.

That personnel had 'strategies of independence' of its own, grounded in the indispensability of its different experts for dealing with public affairs. To the extent that those strategies succeeded, they limited the autonomy of the political class, affecting its ability to offer responsible leadership to the political community.

But the bureaucratization of the state apparatus was over-determined, because it too had been 'pushed' by the democratization of politics. This involved a considerable historical irony. The bureaucratic apparatus was often successful in its drive for autonomy, and, to the extent that its function became less directed by politicians, it formed an obstacle to the full realization of the democratization project, which would have placed accountable politicians in charge of state policy.

The political leader

To overcome this impasse, not so much on behalf of democratic ideals, but of his main political concern – the pursuit of the might and security of the German nation – in *Politics as a Vocation* Weber eloquently projected the image of an effective, responsible political leader. He would definitely live *for* politics, being passionately devoted to the nation's interests. But he would also know how to make use of followers and collaborators who live *from* politics, and how to make the necessary compromises in dealing with circumstances that prevented total attainment of his chosen political objectives. He would also possess the knowledge and experience necessary to avoid being swayed by the arguments of wayward bureaucrats who sought to protect their own economic and status interests. He would be a master of the spoken word, capable of convincing of his own designs first his party's followers, then broader audiences. He would be aware that his *Beruf* might occasionally demand of him choices contrary to conventional, private morality, in particular the choice to deploy the legitimate violence of the state. He would be a member of his party, yet feel responsible towards a whole – the political community, the nation – which transcends that part.

It is clear that Weber loads the figure of a leader, operating in a liberal-democratic context, with demiurgic qualities. He would be rich in personal, charismatic qualities, allowing him to evoke the devotion of his followers, who would focus their political aspirations on him. The constitutional design of the polity would entrust him with all the powers required to secure its internal public order and its external security, even in particularly trying circumstances.

Weber sees the basic feature of a liberal-democratic constitution – the periodic, regular competition between parties for the favour of the electorate – chiefly as a way of selecting the most gifted and committed among competing leaders for the top position. He knows, however, that this is an improbable expectation, given the significance he himself attributes to one regrettably dominant feature of modern society.

Here, administrative arrangements of a bureaucratic nature have become dominant not only within the state and the parties, but also within such different realms of activity as the economy, education, research, medicine or religion. More and more significant social and cultural resources are managed by experts who possess complex and ever-changing technical and scientific information, and who discount the political necessity of intrinsically risky and responsible choices, such as those that politics demands. As a result, modern society increasingly resembles a vast ensemble of diverse bureaucratic hierarchies, within which individuals appear as insignificant cogs. They chiefly pursue their overriding concern for their own security, attentively perform narrower and narrower tasks, seek to gain the favour of their superiors, and avoid personal responsibility by referring to precedents and appealing to directives imparted by others.

The bureaucratic challenge

Weber's awareness of the increasingly significant role of organizational apparatuses, and of the mentality they engender, sometimes imparts an almost tragic undertone to the contrasting themes he occasionally evokes – the themes of charisma, prophecy, leadership, individual initiative and responsibility. At other times, his enduring realistic sense confers an almost banal significance to his views. At the end of *Politics as a Vocation*, for example, he likens politics to the arduous and assiduous labour involved when boring through hard planks of wood – hardly an inspiring image, but certainly a tough-minded one. Politics is frustrating and unrewarding work, but in order to build something worthwhile such labour is necessary, and it requires appropriate skills. It also requires an unusual combination of qualities to perform it day by day without being discouraged by its difficulties, distracted by its details or diverted by its temptations (especially that of vanity). The leader must be passionately committed to the cause, yet realistic in judging the probability of attaining it and in designing the paths to it. He must also be capable of detachment when assessing circumstances. He must be far-seeing, for the willingness to take responsibility for one's choices requires the anticipation of not only their immediate results but also more distant ones, with both wanted and unwanted consequences.

In *Politik als Beruf* this emphasis on the subjective requirements of political experience, in a strong sense of the term, including especially the chief moral component of what Weber called an ethic of responsibility, counterbalances his emphasis in other writings on the objective, institutional aspects of the state, with the breadth and diversity of its tasks, and the complexity of its organization.

In a sense, the relationship posited by Weber between political *Beruf* and political *Betrieb* is an asymmetrical one. Even the state's *Betrieb*, with its tendency to broaden its tasks and absorb and deploy growing resources, rests on a *Beruf* – that of the bureaucrat and the expert. This tendency leads to technocratic temptation, and, as Mannheim suggested, seeks to reduce all politics to administration.

Weber does not specifically describe this tendency. Conceivably, he exercises it by his emphasis on leadership and on the personal qualities it requires, together with the riskiness of the highest political experience, that of the confrontation between sovereign polities, each intent on affirming one nation's interests over and possibly against those of others. After all, he wrote, no bureaucracy is a self-sufficient entity. Each administrative apparatus must take shape and justify itself, initially at least in principle, as the indispensable instrument of a political entity which establishes it and transcends it, and on which it depends. It can, however, avail itself of that indispensability to reduce such dependency as far as possible.

The fact that this bureaucratic tendency increasingly dominates all areas of modern society, not only the political realm, presents a serious challenge. With the growing power of great, complex organizations some values which belong to the very nature of modernity are jeopardized – the values of individuality, of initiative, of risk-taking, of personal autonomy and responsibility. In particular, within capitalism the growing 'managerialization' of enterprises has already reduced the significance of entrepreneurship.

According to a text of Weber's from the last year of the Great War, after the Soviet Revolution, socialism represented this danger in its most extreme form. The socialization of the means of production and the abolition of the market would eliminate the residual space that even a highly 'corporate' economy leaves for those values, for it still compels its units, large as they may be, to compete with one another. Weber was harshly critical concerning the ultimate inhumanity of 'the market' and he never doubted the ethical justifications for the socialist project – under capitalism the class formed by those who sell their 'formally free' labour *is* at a disadvantage vis-à-vis those who buy it. Yet he saw that project as a grave threat to intrinsically modern (and originally Western) values which he held dear, though he knew their validity could not be scientifically proven. He also knew that they were, essentially, 'bourgeois' values. But Max Weber never hesitated to define himself as a 'class-conscious' member of the bourgeoisie.

Select Bibliography

Works by Max Weber

Weber, Max, *Economy and Society*, Berkeley, CA: University of California Press, 1978.

For an up-to-date, extensive bibliography, see:

Sica, Alan (ed.), *Max Weber: A Comprehensive Bibliography*, Brunswick, NJ: Transaction Books, 2004.

There are a number of useful collections of Weberian texts (essays or chapters from books) in English. I would recommend the following:

Gerth, Hans and Mills, C. Wright (eds), *From Max Weber: Essays in Sociology*, New York: Oxford University Press, 1946.

Runciman, Walter G. (ed.), *Max Weber: Selections in Translation*, Cambridge: Cambridge University Press, 1978.

Whimster, Sam (ed.), *The Essential Weber: A Reader*, London: Routledge, 2003.

Works by Max Weber available in English (as 'clusters')

The following list of works available in English is grouped into the 'clusters' provided at the end of chapter 1 (p. 16).

1   Economic history

The History of Commercial Partnerships in the Middle Ages (edited and translated by L. Kaelber), Lanham, MD: Rowman & Littlefield, 2003;

The Agrarian Sociology of Ancient Civilizations (translated by R. I. Frank), London: New Left Books, 1976; *General Economic History* (translated and edited by F. Knight), London: Allen & Unwin, 1927 and Glencoe, IL: Free Press, 1950.

2 Research projects

There are no English translations of the most relevant writings in this cluster.

3 Methodology

Max Weber on the Methodology of the Social Sciences (translated and edited by E. Shils), Glencoe, IL: Free Press, 1949; *Roscher and Knies: The Logical Problems of Historical Economics* (translated and introduced by G. Oakes), New York: Free Press, 1975.

4 Sociology of religion

The Protestant Ethic and the Spirit of Capitalism (translated and edited by T. Parsons), London: Allen & Unwin, 1930 (First published in *Archiv für Sozialwissenschaft und Sozialpolitik*, 1904–5; and in *Gesammelte Aufsätze in Religionssoziologie*, vol. I, Tübingen: Mohr (3 vols), 1920); *The Religion of China: Confucianism and Taoism* (translated and edited by H. Gerth), Glencoe, IL: Free Press, 1951; *The Religion of India: The Sociology of Hinduism and Buddhism* (translated and edited by H. Gerth and D. Martindale), Glencoe, IL: Free Press, 1958; *Ancient Judaism* (translated and edited by H. Gerth and D. Martindale), Glencoe, IL: Free Press, 1952.

5 General sociology

Economy and Society: An Outline of Interpretive Sociology (edited by G. Roth and C. Wittich), Berkeley, CA: University of California Press, 1978.

6 Politics

Weber: Political Writings (edited and translated by P. Lassman and R. Speirs), Cambridge: Cambridge University Press, 1994; *The Russian*

Revolutions (translated and edited by G. Wells and P. Bähr), Ithaca, NY: Cornell University Press, 1995.

Titles in English on Max Weber and his work

Note: The following is a limited selection from a large body of literature. In these books, the reader might look both for further accounts of Weber's own work (not always compatible with the account given in this book) and for indications on the ways in which later authors criticized and/or developed Weber's own ideas.

Albrow, Martin, *Max Weber's Construction of Social Theory*, New York: St Martin's Press, 1990.

Alexander, Jeffrey, *The Classical Attempt at Theoretical Synthesis. Max Weber*, Berkeley, CA: University of California Press, 1983.

Beetham, David, *Max Weber and the Theory of Modern Politics*, London: Allen & Unwin, 1974.

Bendix, Reinhard, *Max Weber: An Intellectual Portrait*, Garden City, NJ: Doubleday, 1960.

Bendix, Reinhard, *The Prince and the Discourses* by Niccolò Machiavelli, with an introduction by Max Lerner, New York: The Modern Library, 1940.

Bendix, Reinhard and Roth, Günther, *Scholarship and Partisanship: Essays on Max Weber*, Berkeley, CA: University of California Press, 1971.

Brubaker, Rogers, *The Limits of Rationality: An Essay on the Social and Moral Thought of Max Weber*, London: Allen & Unwin, 1984.

Burger, Thomas, *Max Weber's Theory of Concept Formation: History, Laws and Ideal Types*, expanded edn, Durham: Duke University Press, 1987.

Collins, Randall, *Weberian Social Theory*, Cambridge: Cambridge University Press, 1986.

Giddens, Anthony, *Politics and Sociology in the Thought of Max Weber*, London: Macmillan, 1972.

Kalberg, Stephen, *Max Weber's Comparative Historical Sociology*, Oxford: Blackwell, 1994.

Kershaw, Ian, *Hitler, 1889–1936*, Hubris, London: Penguin, 1999.

Kronman, Anthony, *Max Weber*, Stanford: Stanford University Press, 1983.

Mommsen, Wolfgang, *The Age of Bureaucracy: Perspectives on the Political Sociology of Max Weber*, Oxford: Blackwell, 1974.

Mommsen, Wolfgang, *Max Weber and German Politics 1890–1920*, Cambridge: Polity, 1989.

Poggi, Gianfranco, *Calvinism and the Capitalist Spirit: Max Weber's 'Protestant Ethic'*, London: Macmillan, 1983.

Roth, Günther and Schluchter, Wolfgang, *Max Weber's Vision of History: Ethics and Methods*, Berkeley, CA: University of California Press, 1979.

Runciman, W.G., *A Critique of Max Weber's Philosophy of Social Science*, Cambridge: Cambridge University Press, 1972.

Schluchter, Wolfgang, *The Rise of Western Rationalism: Max Weber's Developmental History* (translated, with an introduction, by Günther Roth), Berkeley, CA: University of California Press, 1981.

Schluchter, Wolfgang, *Paradoxes of Modernity: Culture and Conduct in the Theory of Max Weber* (translated by Neil Solomon), Stanford: Stanford University Press, 1996.

Swedberg, Richard, *Max Weber and the Idea of Economic Sociology*, Princeton, NJ: Princeton University Press, 1998.

Turner, Bryan, *For Weber: Essays on the Sociology of Fate* (second edn), London: Sage Publications, 1996.

Turner, Stephen (ed.), *The Cambridge Companion to Weber*, Cambridge: Cambridge University Press, 2000.

Turner, Stephen and Factor, Regis, *The Lawyer as Social Thinker*, London: Routledge, 1994.

Weber, Mariann, *Max Weber: A Biography*, New York: Wiley, 1975.

Index

Christianity 76, 77, 80, 85; *see also* Calvinism; Catholic tradition; Protestantism
citizenship 30, 109
city, typology of 30–1
class warfare 19
classes 39, 43–5, 52
coercion, political 89, 90, 94, 109, 110, 115, 123
collective action 55; genesis of 38–9; individualistic perspective 36–8
collective reality 106–7
collective subject 65–8
command, and political power 91, 92–100
communism 33
Communist Manifesto 45, 46
Comte, Auguste 19
Condition of Rural Workers in East-of-the-Elbe Germany (Lage der Landarbeite im ostelbischen Deutschland, Die) 5, 6
conflict 46, 47, 49
Confucianism 16, 76, 80, 81, 82–4; contrasted with Puritanism 84–8
Confucianism and Taoism 81–8, 87
cultural movements 12, 54
cultural sciences: methodology of *see* methodology; Weber's publications 16
culture 77, 80, 90; China 82–3, 86–7

Dante 108
democracy: democratization of politics 10, 118; liberal 113, 119, 122, 124
Descartes, René 55, 79
domination 91; *see also* political power

duty: and capitalist spirit 67; and state 114

Eastern Europe 94
Economic Ethic of the World Religions, The 88
economic history 4–5, 16, 60, 63
economic institutions 60–1
economic power 41, 42, 43, 91
economic resources 52, 109, 114–15
economic science 19
economic sociology, Weber's contribution 60
economic surveys 5, 6, 16
economics 13, 48, 50, 58; Weber as economist 1, 6–7, 59–61; world religions 63, 77–88
Economy and Society 11, 12, 16, 26, 27, 31, 47, 48, 60, 62, 90, 91, 110, 113; charismatic legitimacy in 103; definition of state in 110
Eighteenth Brumaire of Louis Bonaparte (Marx) 108–9
Elias, Norbert 119
end of history 53–4, 56
Engels, Friedrich 19
England *see* Great Britain
entrepreneurship 65–8, 86, 116, 126
erotic experience 13, 50
establishment *see* Betrieb
estates 43–5, 46, 52; polity of the 105, 113
ethnicity 47
Everyman (Scottish play) 85

Fallenstein, Helene *see* Weber, Helene
feminism 9
feudalism 105, 113
first World War 10–12, 89
force *see* coercion

Lightning Source UK Ltd.
Milton Keynes UK
UKHW020044101120
373096UK00006B/440

9 780745 634906